T0013572

Every Memory Deserves Respect

EMDR, the Proven Trauma Therapy
with the Power to Heal

MICHAEL BALDWIN AND **DEBORAH KORN, PsyD**

Copyright © 2021 by Michael Baldwin and Deborah Korn

All rights reserved. No portion of this book may be reproduced—mechanically, electronically, or by any other means, including photocopying—without written permission of the publisher. Published simultaneously in Canada by Thomas Allen & Son Limited.

Library of Congress Cataloging-in-Publication Data is available.

ISBN 978-1-5235-1142-6

Design by Sarah Smith
Cover photo by Sarah Smith

Workman books are available at special discounts when purchased in bulk for premiums and sales promotions as well as for fundraising or educational use. Special editions or book excerpts can also be created to specification. For details, contact the Special Sales Director at specialmarkets@workman.com.

Workman Publishing Co., Inc.
225 Varick Street
New York, NY 10014-4381
workman.com

WORKMAN is a registered trademark of Workman Publishing Co., Inc.

Printed in China
First printing April 2021

10 9 8 7 6 5 4 3 2 1

For my dearest friend Carol,
who loved and supported me right up to her last day on Earth.
—M.W.B.

In memory of Dr. Francine Shapiro,
my mentor and friend, and the developer of EMDR therapy,
who challenged us all to see the possibilities in front of us
and to never, ever give up fighting for what is good and right.
She changed my life and inspired me to help others to change theirs.
—D.L.K.

Contents

Preface // 2

1 What Is This Thing We Call Trauma? // 8

2 How Does Trauma Affect Your Mind, Body,
and Behavior? // 54

3 How Does Trauma Affect Your Brain? // 109

4 What Is EMDR Therapy, and How Does It Work? // 148

5 Contemplating Treatment: Am I Ready?
Can I Really Do This? // 212

6 Keeping Your Eye on the Prize:
The Promise of Transformation // 234

7 When You're Ready:
Resources to Get You Started on Your EMDR Journey // 249

Epilogue // 267

Debbie's Recommended Resources // 274

Notes // 278

Acknowledgments // 285

Appendix // 289

Photo Credits // 292

Index // 294

Trauma is a part of life.
It need not be a
source of shame.

Preface

Michael: The inspiration for this book was simple: I experienced trauma during my childhood and recovered from it with EMDR therapy, so I wanted to speak to people who might also be trauma survivors, to let them know that there's hope for healing in their lives, too. I also wanted to give them a guide for how to get there. Most important, I wanted people to understand that trauma is *a part of life*—it need not carry stigma or be a source of shame.

As I experienced the various phases of treatment, I developed a conceptual understanding of what trauma is and why it sometimes gets locked in our brains but outside our day-to-day awareness. I came to recognize the symptoms and red flags associated with trauma, the survival strategies we develop to cope with pain, and much more. I also developed firsthand knowledge of what EMDR therapy is—and how it can be used to help us heal.

Each chapter of this book has been written to communicate various concepts as I came to understand them during my own recovery. We have shared them in two ways: in an immediate and visual way, through photographs—because people are far more likely to understand and remember a concept when text is combined with images—and through my own narrative. In addition, I've had the honor of collaborating with Dr. Deborah Korn, a leading trauma expert, who describes the core concepts of trauma and EMDR therapy in a clear and nonclinical voice.

I hope this book will inspire other trauma survivors to seek relief through therapy like I did, so they, too, can find a path to their authentic selves and live the lives they deserve.

Our memories—even fragments of memories—are *clues*. Like a trail of breadcrumbs. They might be incomplete or confusing at first. But if we have the courage to face the ones that scare us the most, they can lead to discoveries that will free us.

Our memories are the caretakers of truth in our lives.

And *every memory* deserves respect.

Michael Baldwin

Debbie: On a weekly basis, it's not uncommon for me to reach for a book on my shelf with the intention of handing it to a client who is having a hard time with something. I love books and have a huge array of texts that were written for clients new to therapy and, more specifically, for trauma survivors. I offer books in the hope of providing some education, some inspiration, and some validation, and a new framework for understanding symptoms and struggles. More often than not, though, my clients look at me and then at the book in my hand and say, "Thanks, but no thanks." They often feel overwhelmed just looking at the cover, the size of the print, and the number of pages. Some even ask playfully, "Are there any pictures?" Because concentration in day-to-day life is already quite difficult for many of my clients, reading a book is not something they necessarily embrace as a pleasurable activity. Especially a book about trauma!

When Michael contacted me and shared his vision for this book, I jumped at the opportunity to join him on his "survivor mission." I was delighted with his proposal—his enthusiasm was contagious and his personal story compelling. I was touched by his deep desire to educate others about the value of good trauma treatment. Michael explained that EMDR therapy, experienced within the security of his relationship with Jeffrey J. Magnavita, PhD, had offered him a new lease on life. As a result of his experience, he wanted to make sure that others who were suffering, particularly those who had endured abuse and neglect in childhood, knew about everything that EMDR therapy and good trauma treatment, more generally, can offer.

From our very first meeting, I was moved by Michael's sincere desire to bring hope and information to others who might benefit from trauma-focused psychotherapy. I was excited to learn that he had spent most of his professional life in marketing and advertising; as a result, he had a treasure trove of innovative ideas related to the goal of getting needed trauma-focused information and guidance out to the public. His interest in combining poignant text with visuals seemed like a powerful and novel idea. I started to envision creating a book that my clients might actually read! In time, we started to play with the notion of producing a book that might also appeal to therapists, primary care doctors, employee assistance professionals, educators, and even lawyers and probation officers. We imagined these professionals sharing this book with the people in their care.

Throughout *Every Memory Deserves Respect*, I have incorporated the words and stories of my own clients to bring certain concepts and emotional struggles to life. Michael and I hope that we have succeeded in creating a book that challenges you to be courageous and fierce about your recovery, gives you hope, and inspires you to embark or continue on a journey that will potentially change your life in ways that you perhaps can't even imagine right now.

Deborah Korn, PsyD

Trigger Warnings: *Every Memory Deserves Respect* is a book about trauma. As such, we will be touching on some common sources of trauma and Michael will be sharing his own story, including some details about what he experienced as a child. Also, Debbie will be recounting the healing journeys of some of her clients. Potentially triggering material can be found in the middle of page 11, and on pages 201 and 205. If you are feeling overstimulated or if you anticipate having a hard time with material being presented, skip those pages. Please, please take good care of yourself. And in the spirit of this book, if you find yourself struggling in any way as you read, take note of what is triggering you and think about bringing that information to your therapist or sharing it with someone close to you.

In research spanning twenty-four countries on six continents, 70 percent of adults reported one or more traumas in their lifetime.

1

What Is This Thing We Call Trauma?

Michael: I grew up in an affluent family, and an outsider might assume that I had everything I ever wanted or needed. But all my life, I felt lost, like I had nothing, that I *was* nothing. At the age of sixty-one, despite years of therapy, I was no closer to understanding why so many things that came effortlessly to others were impossible for me: sustaining a relationship or a career, even using a public restroom. When I arrived for my first therapy session with Dr. Jeffrey Magnavita in March 2017, I was so overcome by panic and phobias that my life felt like a prison.

Over the course of my treatment, I was able to unravel my story. To help you understand my journey, I'll present it as I initially knew it, and then tell you how I eventually came to comprehend it, experience it, and make it my own.

My parents married right out of college—Sarah Lawrence for my mother and Yale for my father. They moved to Indianapolis, Indiana, where they had their first child—my brother—and then to Denver, Colorado, where they immediately had three more children in three years: my older sister, me in 1955, and then my younger sister. My mother was pregnant again just eight weeks after my brother was born, and by the time she was twenty-nine, she had two toddlers and two infants in the house. Although nothing excuses what came later, I cannot imagine the physical and emotional toll that must have taken on her.

Despite the sudden explosive growth of our family, our homes in Colorado and then Piedmont, California, were gorgeous—as were my parents. My father was tall, slim, and handsome. My mother was equally attractive and charismatic. And everything in our homes was beautifully appointed. Some of my earliest memories remain vivid today, like wanting to show off my mother's beauty and style at elementary school functions, and shopping for the clothes she loved to dress me in.

All that was true.

It's also true that my parents were a terrible match. They never should have gotten married. My mother thought that she had married a prince—handsome face and appearance, good family name. What she got was a wanderer, with no self-confidence and no idea how to operate in an adult world. My father was a lost philosopher. The packaging was deceptive and didn't reflect who he was on the inside. My parents were young, drank heavily, fought often, and paid their four children little attention, regularly leaving us to fend for ourselves—and to antagonize one another.

I don't know the entirety of what my older brother's experience was of my parents, but by the time I was born, he was angry enough, or perhaps just frustrated enough by the cries of an unattended baby wailing for his mother, to regularly torment me. When I was very small, I lived in fear that he would try to smother me when no one was looking. And as I became an active preschooler, he'd frequently sit on my ribs and hit my chest with his fists. From a very early age, I experienced the anguish of being ignored by my parents and bullied by my brother.

My mother would frequently leave us unattended at home for hours at a time, and I'd often be put out in the backyard with no supervision. In a diaper and barefoot, I'd wander out of the yard and make my way to the traffic intersection near our house, where I'd stay until a neighbor would find me and bring me back. My mother laughed about this over the years. However, when I grew up and started to imagine my nieces or nephews being allowed to wander off at age two or three, I began to understand how neglected I had been.

As for my own part in the household dynamic—when my little sister came along, I took out my frustration and pain on her; I felt guilty for many years for bullying her just as my brother had bullied me. In talking with my siblings as adults, I have come to realize that none of us ever felt relaxed or safe growing up in that household.

I also suffered multiple concussions as a child, probably six by the first grade. My mother explained it away as my being "accident-prone," but looking back, I think it was a combination of my hyperactivity, tendency to daydream or dissociate, and an unwitting attempt to get some attention from my mother. She started taping bulky pieces of carpeting to my forehead—to protect me, possibly, yes, but also to announce to the world that her son was handicapped in some way. It left me feeling humiliated and ashamed. I have many pictures of myself over those years, out in public with different types of carpeting taped to my forehead. Like a freak.

My father seemed to adore my brother, who was quite athletic and stereotypically masculine, whereas he didn't seem to like me much, perhaps because I was not the football- or baseball-playing kind of son he wanted. I sometimes thought that what he didn't like about me was exactly what he despised about himself. In turn, he wanted to snuff out or beat out the different, more creative parts of me. Had I been admitted to Deerfield Academy, the prep school he went to and loved, he would have shipped me off no questions asked, because he thought the experience would transform me into the kind of boy I should have been. As it turned out, I escaped that fate because my test scores were so poor. I had way more energy than he could handle, and a very creative spirit. Although there were some similarities between us, I was actually quite different from him, and that probably bothered him, too.

He paid me little attention outside of belittling me or beating me with one of his two Yale oak fraternity paddles, pants down and bare bottom. I can still hear the sound those two paddles would make, knocking against each other, when he'd reach for one of them, and can remember the fear that sound immediately triggered in me.

As we grew, my father seemed determined to prevent both my brother and me from excelling in any way. He gave us the clear but unspoken message, "You better not surpass me. You better not eclipse me. You better not upstage me—or else."

I was first taken to a therapist when I was in the third grade because my mother could see that I was struggling in school, getting no interest or attention from my father, and being bullied by my brother. I remember having conversations with the therapist and reacting to pictures of Rorschach inkblots—what I now recognize as part of a psychological evaluation to assess my emotional functioning. At the end of my evaluation, the therapist told me I was unhappy. I, however, insisted that I was *happy*, that there was nothing wrong with me, and that I didn't need to return. This was the beginning of the construction of the persona of Happy Michael, the one who fit the image that my family projected outwardly.

I also remember from around that age the beginning of a fixation on the exterior markers of status and belonging. On my ninety-minute bus commute to and from school in San Francisco, I would lose myself in my favorite comic book series, Richie Rich, and live vicariously in Richie's world of outsized, cartoon-exaggerated wealth, privilege, and status—but also safety and security.

At school, things were no easier. Reading, comprehension, and retention were nearly impossible for me. I would start reading a paragraph, my mind would wander, and I would have to start over and over, again and again. My brother got nearly straight As with seemingly little effort; I got mostly Cs and had to go to a special reading school after the normal school day, and had reading and math tutors on the weekends. I was also the target of the class bully, who would seek me out to tease and torment me. One day, while I was standing in the lunch line, he punched me in the stomach so hard, I passed out. I woke up lying on the floor, looking up at a circle of faces, feeling ashamed and embarrassed. I couldn't defend myself at home or at school, and it frequently felt like there was no place where I was liked or even tolerated.

My parents divorced when I was fourteen. As I got older, my relationship with my mother shifted. Outside our home, she was overtly flirtatious with other men. With me, she lacked boundaries and it felt like she was sexualizing our relationship. She would leave the door partly open when she changed or showered. She'd frequently ask me to zip up the back of her dress, and I remember an overwhelming feeling of paralyzed revulsion, thinking, *No, I don't want this. I do not want to see my mother like this.* But being asked to zip her up was better than being ignored. I desperately wanted a connection with my mother, so I disregarded my own needs and the sense of violation that came with her lack of boundaries.

After I graduated from Piedmont High School and went on to college, eager to get away from all this, I was dismayed to find that my psychological struggles only intensified.

Over the next forty-plus years, as I moved from Boston to Los Angeles and then New York City and built my career in advertising, I saw six different therapists. As my peers fell in love, got married, and started families, I remained alone, with no idea what it meant to be truly attached or in love as an adult. I distracted myself from my loneliness by relentlessly seeking status and recognition. I wasn't motivated to achieve, I was *compelled* to. But no achievement, no matter how spectacular, was ever enough. The satisfaction always faded, and I then moved on to the next, bigger, loftier goal.

How did I feel, living like this? Like a rat who learns how to tap a bar for food. Every high was short-lived, so I was driven to keep tapping, desperate to receive something more. I had to do/get/wear/be *more* to sustain the feeling of importance and acceptance and to keep the dark feelings at bay. But sadly, none of it provided any real foundation of security or confidence—it was a façade that would completely collapse with one comment from a friend, family member, or client suggesting that I had fallen short in some way. *I'm no good; I'm a fraud; I'm a failure; I don't belong; I'm going to get fired; I'm going to run out of money; I'll end up homeless in the streets; I'll die lonely and alone.*

On the outside, I had the best job, the best apartment, the best clothes. But inside, I felt small and fragile. Any situation related to intimacy with a woman—even the contemplation of it—filled me with panic and the urge to run away as fast as I could. I tried my best to fit in and engage in a world that, to me, felt alien and scary. But when a date invited me back to her apartment, I would seize up

There is no escaping the gravity of trauma.

No distraction—not money, fame, or achievement— can insulate you.

in complete terror, as if my life were in immediate danger. Once, when a female friend visiting for the weekend surprised me by coming downstairs to my bedroom late at night in her nightgown, I froze. Completely immobilized, I could barely speak. I think I zoned out at the time, because after the weekend, I couldn't quite remember what had happened after the initial shock of seeing her in that nightgown. I didn't understand what was happening to me and feared that I was going crazy.

In my day-to-day life, traveling the world for my job, I dreaded the possibility of having to use a public restroom. Since childhood, just the thought of entering a public restroom brought on real anxiety, which could quickly turn into acute panic. As irrational as this sounds, I feared that I would be exposed and vulnerable in a bathroom stall and that someone would climb over or under the stall door and somehow hurt me. I also had recurring nightmares that left me shaking and soaked with sweat. In one, I fell, night after night, from the top of the Empire State Building and crashed onto the sidewalk below. I had no idea what it meant. Any proximity to heights, railings, bridges, or observation decks provoked an intense tightening and knotting in my body.

So, I avoided it all—intimate relationships, public bathrooms, heights, and any kind of vulnerability or authentic engagement with other human beings. Personally and professionally, I limited any and all potential for spontaneity, satisfaction, and joy, shrinking my life in search of an ever-elusive sense of safety.

Then in 2003, because of the unexpected loss of an account, I was laid off by my advertising agency, Ogilvy & Mather. I had spent my entire career *dreaming* about working there, and for the previous seven years, it had been my home. That sudden loss sent me into a total tailspin.

I lost my emotional anchor and the much-needed distraction of my high-status job. As a result, I found myself in a state of constant terror about money. I was convinced that I was going to end up homeless—and then proceeded to make a series of disastrous financial decisions that brought me to that brink. I had to sell my car, my apartment, and all of my furnishings. Eventually, I used up nearly all of my savings. Unable to sleep at night, I began drinking heavily so I could just pass out. I started having alcoholic blackouts, waking up with no idea how I'd gotten home the night before.

Still hungry for approval and attention and with no real possibilities for getting those needs met in a healthy way, I became overly involved in my mother's life, spending hours on the phone trying to meet *her* needs—troubleshooting her internet problems, setting up doctor's appointments and medical procedures for her, and trying to keep her happy in any way I could.

Meanwhile, I was wearing out my two sisters and my brother, calling them way too often to rehash all my anxieties and uncertainty.

Unable to conduct my life in accordance with the compulsive, goal-set/goal-achieve pattern that had previously *defined* me, I was paralyzed. I couldn't think clearly and had lost any and all sense of creativity and capacity for self-reflection. I couldn't move forward, and I couldn't make sense of how the past had led me to the present. I was more miserable than I'd thought possible.

And still—after decades of therapy—I had no idea why.

Debbie: I have been interested in trauma since the earliest days of my education. In my early clinical work, I found that no matter what issues brought people into treatment, nine times out of ten there was some kind of trauma story behind it. Since then,

Phobias are often a telltale sign of trauma.

my teaching, research, writing, and day-to-day clinical work have all focused on helping people who have endured painful trauma in their lives, typically starting at an early age. I began to see patterns—both in the ways that our brains deal with trauma and in the ways that people attempt to cope with the aftereffects of devastating life experiences. I began to see what helped people heal—and what didn't.

In 1987, psychologist Francine Shapiro made a discovery during a walk in the park. While walking, she was thinking about some recent disturbing events in her life. As she considered these events, she became aware that her eyes were moving back and forth. As her eyes moved, she noticed that the negative emotional charge of the painful memories that had driven her to the park that day subsided dramatically. She began exploring the connection between "bilateral" (back-and-forth) eye movements and the diminishing or "desensitization" of anxiety. She eventually developed a full treatment around this feature and conducted controlled research and case studies to evaluate its effects. She named the approach Eye Movement Desensitization—EMD—and later changed the name to EMDR—Eye Movement Desensitization and *Reprocessing* therapy. That's exactly what it is—a psychotherapy for desensitizing anxiety (taking away or lowering distress) and reprocessing traumatic memories. And yes, it's also a mouthful and an earful. We know.

What Dr. Shapiro came to prove was that trauma victims are actually able to experience a reduction in symptoms and start experiencing a level of peace and healing within a few sessions. Previously, this kind of change had been possible only after years of talk therapy—if ever.

Subsequently, EMDR has been intensively studied and proven effective—and efficient—in the treatment of post-traumatic stress disorder (PTSD). PTSD develops in response to a traumatic experience that causes intense fear, helplessness, or horror. EMDR therapy is recognized as an effective form of treatment for PTSD by the American Psychiatric Association, the World Health Organization, the International Society for Traumatic Stress Studies, and the US Departments of Veterans Affairs and Defense. More than a hundred thousand clinicians throughout the world use the therapy, and millions of people have been treated successfully over the past thirty years.

Before EMDR therapy, it was widely assumed that severe emotional pain requires a long time to heal. Extensive research has shown EMDR to be an effective form of treatment for post-traumatic stress disorder, with up to 90 percent of adults who experienced a single traumatic event no longer presenting with PTSD after only three ninety-minute sessions. Research also supports the use of EMDR therapy with people who have experienced repeated trauma, including significant forms of child abuse and neglect. In an important early EMDR study, 77 percent of traumatized combat veterans were free of PTSD in just twelve sessions. And in another early study at a medical and psychiatric treatment center, 100 percent of single-trauma and 77 percent of multiple-trauma survivors no longer met the diagnostic criteria for PTSD after six fifty-minute EMDR sessions. This study concluded that EMDR was, without question, more effective than the center's "standard care" in reducing the symptoms of PTSD, coexisting depression, and anxiety. A recent meta-analysis found that EMDR was not only clinically effective but also the most cost-effective of the eleven trauma therapies evaluated in the treatment of adults with PTSD.

EMDR therapy allows us to efficiently clear out traumatic memories that have gotten stuck in our brains.

I had the honor of consulting on a study funded by the National Institute of Mental Health that evaluated the effects of eight sessions of EMDR therapy compared with eight weeks of taking Prozac for the treatment of PTSD. EMDR was superior for reducing both PTSD symptoms and depression. By the end of treatment, 100 percent of those traumatized as adults had lost their PTSD diagnosis, and 73 percent of those with childhood trauma histories no longer had a PTSD diagnosis. At a six-month follow-up, with no additional EMDR therapy beyond the initial eight sessions, 89 percent of the childhood abuse survivors had lost their PTSD diagnosis. Furthermore, 33 percent were considered completely asymptomatic.

Once traumatic experiences and their related triggers have been processed, we expect to see a reduction or even a complete remission in a wide range of problems and symptoms. In addition to applications with obvious trauma-related problems and diagnoses, EMDR is being used to treat people of all ages—who may or may not have PTSD—suffering from depression, anxiety, phobias, pain, eating disorders, addictions, psychotic disorders, and medically unexplained physical symptoms. It's being used with combat veterans and first responders (police, firefighters, EMTs, doctors, and nurses) as well as with groups of people in the immediate aftermath of "critical incidents" or disasters, such as mass shootings, hurricanes and floods, and terrorist attacks. With EMDR therapy at my disposal during the coronavirus pandemic, I was able to effectively and efficiently treat frontline workers (employed in grocery stores, hospitals, and homeless shelters), those who had been on ventilators in the ICU, and those who had suffered devastating losses of loved ones.

EMDR therapy is based on the idea that psychological difficulties are related to the brain's failure to adequately process traumatic memories. Of course, most mental health experts support the notion that past experiences have at least something to do with our current personalities, coping styles, relationship difficulties, and psychological struggles. This idea is certainly not new. However, EMDR therapy *specifically* searches for and addresses memories related to current dysfunction. As memories are adequately processed with EMDR, symptoms recede and memories get more effectively connected to other related memories and information, allowing shifts in thoughts, feelings, behaviors, and physical sensations. Healing involves spontaneous movement toward positive thinking and more manageable feelings, and a significant reduction in distress and anxiety experienced in one's body.

The theory behind EMDR argues that the mind can heal from psychological trauma in the same way the body heals from physical trauma; we are all physiologically geared toward the achievement of optimal health. If you have been physically injured and left with a wound, the body will naturally and spontaneously mobilize to heal that wound. The body may need a little help removing barriers (i.e., infection) to healing, but it clearly knows what to do.

When people come into treatment, typically their world is quite small. They have pulled back because so many things in their day-to-day experience and relationships with other people have become "triggers" for them, activating overwhelming emotions and distress. They are feeling isolated, or hopeless, or defective. But what I have always loved about this work is that *people get better*. With all that we know today about effective treatment, I can confidently say to a client in the first session, "You were injured—perhaps in many different ways, emotionally, physically, sexually—but you can recover. This is not something you were born with or need to keep living with. We will do the work, together, and

Our mind can heal from psychological trauma like our body heals from physical trauma.

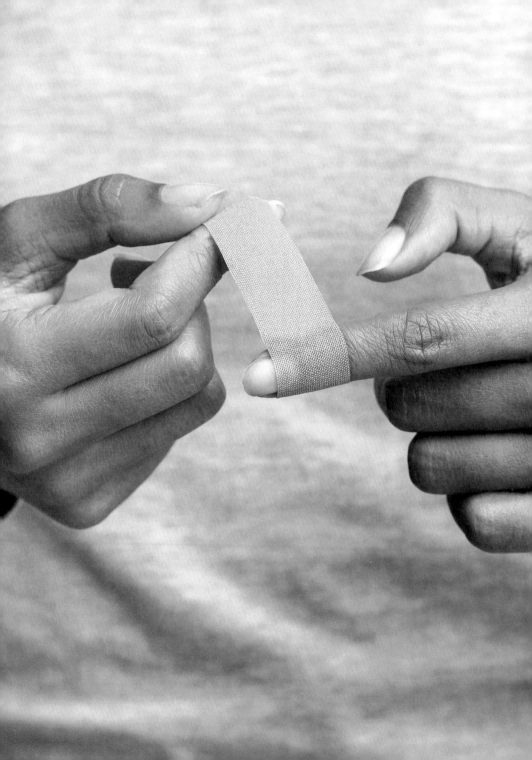

you will heal." That, to me, is an incredibly hopeful and wonderful way to start a journey with someone.

Before learning EMDR, I spent years treating trauma survivors with various other approaches but was far from satisfied with the results I was getting. In 1992, when I introduced EMDR to my out-patient and inpatient clients at a large, private psychiatric hospital, I quickly became convinced that this novel treatment promised a level of healing like nothing I had ever seen before. Several decades later, EMDR therapy remains my treatment of choice, and I am excited to tell you all about it. But before Michael and I can take you through how EMDR heals, it's vital for you to understand what trauma actually is—and isn't—and what typically needs healing in the aftermath of traumatic experiences. We'll begin in these first three chapters by defining trauma and unpacking the relationships between trauma and one's mind, body, brain, behavior, heart, and spirit. And then, in chapter 4, we'll dive into the nuts and bolts of EMDR therapy.

WHAT IS TRAUMA?

From our very first skinned knee, we all understand that traumatic physical events may cause bruises or breaks. They leave scars that can be seen. Most of us also understand that certain kinds of events leave mental scars that cannot necessarily be seen. We can grasp why a veteran might have combat-related nightmares and flash-backs, why a rape victim might be fearful about leaving home at night unaccompanied, or why a survivor of a serious car accident might get panicky thinking about driving on the highway. However, less commonly understood is the reality that emotional events can also have lasting, measurable effects on one's mind, brain, and behavior. Our brains evolved to perform one key task: keeping us alive to pass on our genes. Unfortunately, the hardwiring for how to do that evolved hundreds of thousands of years ago and has not yet been updated to version 2.0.

One way we survived was by holding on to memories of threatening experiences so we would know to avoid them in the future. Think about it in the most basic of terms. If eating a particular red berry made you sick, your brain made sure you remembered that fact. Forgetting the threats in your environment, or getting lax in your response to the danger, could get you killed. Although not all red berries were dangerous, the world was, in fact, a dangerous place, and our evolution favored holding on to the memories of all potential dangers and never letting go. Following the adage "Better safe than sorry," we learned to avoid all red berries. But at some point, getting a warning from our nervous system to go on high alert every single time we see a reminder of an earlier, traumatic event—every time we see a red berry or maybe even a berry of any color—stops making sense. The "Danger!" label that our brain assigned to red berries may no longer be warranted.

Think about the reactions you've experienced or witnessed in others—anxious, embarrassed, sad, or angry responses to seemingly benign or even positive situations such as receiving recognition, surprise parties, or friendly competitions. Or, in more challenging situations, reactions that have seemed extreme or somehow out of place—severe depression after a breakup, rage in response to a coworker's mistake, or terror upon losing a job. All you know is that these responses seem somehow out of proportion to the event at hand. These may very well reflect a memory frozen in the brain at the time of some earlier trauma, still throwing up red flags years, or even decades, later. It's safe to assume that none of the

Potentially traumatic experiences include:

Death of a loved one

Being fired or laid off

Bankruptcy

Foreclosure

Abandonment

Divorce

Witnessing terror

Natural disaster

Miscarriage

Suicide of a family
member or friend

Illness or injury

Addiction of a family
member or friend

Ridicule

Humiliation

Failure

Inability to protect
or save someone

Neglect

Betrayal

Poverty

Deprivation

Bullying

Domestic violence

Car accident

Assault

Robbery

Living in fear

Emotional abuse

Physical abuse

Sexual abuse

War

Terrorism

Combat

Genocide

Physical confrontation

Sexual harassment

Discrimination

Racism

Prejudice

Being objectified

Rejection

Pandemic stress

women who invited Michael back to their dorm rooms intended him any harm. But his brain detected some kind of threat and did what it was hardwired to do: It activated his amygdala, the part of the brain that responds to threat, and sent him into a fight-or-flight response.

This is because our clever, survival-wired brains lock traumatic memories away with all of their component parts—images and other sensory input, feelings, thoughts and beliefs, and sensations—intact and relatively unchanged. And these memories remain stuck in our nervous system, waiting to be recalled whenever a reactivating trigger—any event or experience that is similar in some way to an older memory—comes along.

Components of a Memory

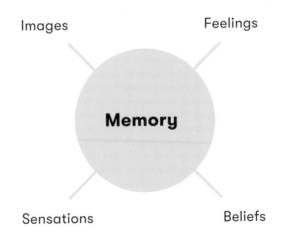

Images

Feelings

Memory

Sensations

Beliefs

The trigger can be a sound, a smell, or a physical sensation; a rejection, a perceived failure, or a loss. Or a feeling: fear, shame, guilt, grief, or anger. Maybe a thought like *I'm stupid* or *I'm helpless.* And this triggering can happen a day after the initial event, a month later, or years later. Sometimes the whole memory comes back, but often, since traumatic memories get stored as fragments, it's just a piece. Suddenly we feel emotionally or physically hijacked— experiencing a reaction that seems to come out of left field. Maybe we find ourselves in tears or totally enraged, or running away, shutting down, or getting foggy. Something in our current situation has reactivated the frozen memory of a traumatic experience in our nervous system, stimulating a thought, a feeling, a sensation, a behavioral reaction—or a full-blown flashback.

Thanks, evolution. Please let us know when the new operating system is available.

Trauma Is Not Exclusively the Event

When trying to understand trauma, it is perhaps most important to understand that it isn't simply defined by an event. Yes, there are some events—what we might refer to as "big-*T*" traumas—such as combat or terrorist attacks, domestic or community violence, serious accidents, natural disasters, sexual or physical abuse, life-threatening illnesses, and unexpected losses—that would deeply affect most anyone. In the broadest sense, though, the term *trauma* can refer to any experience that feels overwhelming, triggers strong negative emotions, or involves a sense of powerlessness and intense vulnerability.

With this definition in mind, trauma would also be the appropriate term for emotional abuse and any experiences involving rejection, humiliation, failure, abandonment, neglect, discrimination, or prejudice. Trauma might also come with a divorce, losing a job, a difficult move, or the discovery of your partner's affair. And certainly, in childhood, feeling ignored, criticized, unable to measure up to parents' expectations or siblings' triumphs, or regularly feeling alone and utterly isolated can have a huge effect on your sense of well-being. Therapists often refer to these kinds of experiences as "little-*t*" traumas. Everyone experiences little-*t* events. If you are human, you know what I'm talking about here. Things happen. You tell yourself they shouldn't be a big deal, but they are. They feel hard to let go of or shake—and before you know it, they spontaneously link to other experiences that have affected you in similar ways. You say to yourself, *See, I am stupid. I don't stand a chance of making it in the world. I'm doomed for failure.* Over time, the cumulative effect of little-*t* traumas on physical and mental health and your sense of identity can be quite serious and debilitating.

When we are dealt something beyond what we can handle, no matter how big or small, together with the belief that there's little or nothing we can do about it, the brain—without consulting us—grabs that experience, registers what is most important about it from a survival perspective, and sets it aside, locking it in its own little compartment. And if it doesn't get attended to or properly processed mentally or emotionally (we'll explain this in greater detail later), there it remains, just beneath the surface—bearing influence, shaping decisions and reactions, and, at times, causing significant symptoms that interfere with our ability to function. So, bottom line: A trauma isn't just what happens to you; it's actually more about what happens *within* you—in your mind, brain, and body. Trauma is both objective *and* subjective.

Most people who experience a traumatic event in their adult years, even if they have some kind of acute stress reaction

Traumatic experiences remain preserved in the brain and body, often unaltered from the moment they occurred.

immediately after an incident, do not move on to develop PTSD. In fact, only about 20 percent of adult trauma survivors do. Many different factors influence one's response to trauma and the likelihood of developing a psychiatric disorder: age, temperament, family dynamics and level of social support, intensity and duration of the trauma exposure, genetics, and various resilience factors. Traumatized children and adolescents are much more likely to develop PTSD than traumatized adults. Young children, because of their diminutive size and strength, reliance on adults, and vulnerability are the age group most likely to be abused; adolescents are next. When we encounter terrible, overwhelming experiences in childhood, a time when we are by nature powerless or limited in our ability to exert control, we are much more vulnerable to the damaging effects of trauma. That is why I am always reminding my clients that they can't judge their actions from childhood by their present-day, adult standards. The needs and capacities of a ten-year-old are very different from those of a mature grown-up.

When people come into therapy with me, part of my initial evaluation involves asking them about their history. It is very common for people to minimize or dismiss experiences that I might consider significant or traumatic. Frequently I suspect, because of the way they tell their story—with little eye contact, trepidation or hesitation in their voice, a knee that never stops bouncing, and hands that are twisting—that an experience was, indeed, traumatic for them. For many, it seems that their traumatic past is still with them, in their minds and in their bodies. Yet possibly the most common thing I hear early in therapy is "But doesn't everyone go through something like this?" or "I don't think I had it any worse than anyone else." Often people will say, "I don't know why I was so sensitive," or "It wasn't so bad—I just didn't handle it well," attributing their injury to an inadequacy within themselves rather than to the devastating nature of the event, the other person, or the lack of support in their lives.

Complex Interpersonal Trauma:
Getting Hurt Repeatedly by People You Know

Complex interpersonal trauma is the most pervasive form of trauma that I hear about in my practice. By *complex* we mean stressors or traumas that are repetitive, prolonged, and most often, cumulative. *Interpersonal* means the trauma is experienced at the hands of one or more people; it is typically, but not always, deliberate and includes all forms of victimization, exploitation, and maltreatment (emotional, physical, and sexual abuse and neglect). When the trauma occurs within a relationship where there is an intimate bond or a sense of dependency (parent-child, doctor-patient, athlete-coach, marriage or romantic relationship), we might also refer to it as attachment or relational trauma. And when it occurs in childhood, during the formative years of development, it is often referred to as developmental trauma. This kind of trauma was the cornerstone of Michael's experience.

I see individuals who grew up enduring emotional, physical, or sexual abuse over prolonged periods of time at the hands of alcoholic, drug-addicted, mentally ill, or neglectful parents, or from parents who themselves were trauma survivors and too dysfunctional or out of control to parent effectively. Michael and I have discussed the fact that his father was a Korean War veteran, who perhaps had his own undiagnosed PTSD. Sometimes trauma survivors were raised by caregivers who were incredibly frightening. And sometimes their caregivers were frightened themselves, as in domestic-violence or high-conflict situations.

When a child is hurt, betrayed, or abandoned by an adult they depend on, the damage is significantly worse than being hurt by a stranger. It's important to note, too, that trauma is created not just by acts of commission—the things that happen to us. It is also created by acts of *omission*, such as neglect, deprivation, lack of support, or lack of adult comfort and nurturing, all of which can produce a sense of profound and utter aloneness, unworthiness, and hopelessness.

Often I hear things like, "When I was a kid, I came home to an empty house [or apartment or trailer], made myself a sandwich, if there was food, and watched TV. If I did see my mother, she was sleeping in her bedroom or passed out on the floor. For years, that was the story of my life." I see with my clients that it's easy for them to minimize their trauma if they've experienced "only" deprivation, neglect, or psychological abuse. But when you grow up without a sense of security, when you grow up fending for yourself, it dramatically affects the developing brain, your experience of yourself, and your sense of the world around you.

For many, childhood traumas are then followed by adult traumas. Research clearly shows that childhood sexual abuse survivors are at greater risk of victimization at later points in their lives than those without this kind of early exposure to abuse. Almost half of these survivors are sexually victimized again in the future. Growing up in environments without resources, protection, supports, or models, survivors often fail to learn how to properly protect themselves, how to establish good boundaries, or how to make good choices in terms of relationships. Without these skills, people are likely to engage in significant risk taking or put themselves into situations where there is a higher probability of harm. Many of them never learned to recognize the warning signs of danger or that they could say "Stop" or "No" or "Ouch." Sometimes, they choose inappropriate partners or put up with awful bosses because they don't believe themselves worthy of anything better or deserving of more than what they're getting; they're happy to settle for leftover crumbs because that's what they've been doing their whole lives.

The Role of Early Attachment

The term *attachment* refers to the physiological and emotional bond between two people, initially an infant and caregiver, that establishes the template for all future relationships. "Attachment injuries" harm children by destroying their sense of psychological well-being and safety and by limiting the development of their self-esteem and their capacity to deal effectively with their emotions and interactions with others. When there are significant and repeated ruptures or failures in early relationships with caregivers, children learn that they are worthless, damaged, unloved, unwanted, dispensable, and of value only in meeting others' needs. Rather than the voice of a loving, supportive caregiver in their hearts and minds, they hear a critical or shaming voice from within. Or, there is no voice *at all* to calm their anxiety or cheer them on in the face of challenges. It is noteworthy that in 2012, the American Academy of Pediatrics released a special report recognizing psychological maltreatment as the most challenging and prevalent form of child abuse and neglect. In numerous studies published by prominent researchers, it is dramatically clear that emotional abuse and neglect carry greater "weight" than other widely recognized forms of child abuse. Children and adolescents with psychological maltreatment, such as parental verbal abuse, in their backgrounds consistently show equal or worse clinical

One secure attachment
can make all the difference
in the emotional
development of a child.

outcome profiles than kids with exposure to both physical and sexual abuse.

This ties into the very definition of trauma. If children lack a healthy adult presence—someone who can hold their hand, explain things, and offer comfort in the aftermath of an event—then many events that otherwise might not have been traumatic become experiences that overwhelm their senses and create a pronounced sense of powerlessness and devastation. For example, after the death of a beloved grandparent, a child who has a parent to explain things, listen, and comfort may not experience the loss as a trauma. It would be experienced as a sad experience, but not as something that leaves them feeling alone and powerless and confused, and not as something that goes on to affect their nervous system and relationships for years into the future.

We form a secure attachment when, as an infant or child, we learn we can depend on an attuned, predictable, safe, and loving caregiver. An attuned adult reads and responds to both verbal ("I need you; I don't like this") and nonverbal (sad face, withdrawal, crying) cues. These cues communicate core emotions (I'm sad and scared), physical or emotional states (I'm hungry, tired, and lonely), and needs (I need to be comforted, held, played with, listened to). With the kinds of experiences that come with healthy attachments, little ones learn to better tolerate stress (from the outside) and distress (on the inside) and, over time, develop their own capacity for self-regulation. According to Karlen Lyons-Ruth, a developmental psychologist and professor of psychology at Harvard Medical School, "The attachment system can be thought of as the psychological version of the immune system." Secure attachment combats and reduces stress in the same way the immune system fights physical disease. She reports that without this foundation of security, people are more vulnerable to getting derailed by trauma and remain significantly handicapped in their ability to self-regulate and recover from their psychological wounds.

Braking and Accelerating: Trauma and Its Effect on Self-Regulation

To understand the concept of self-regulation, consider our internal thermostat. When you are too hot or cold, your body makes minor adjustments to regulate your temperature until you are once again in a comfortable, optimal zone. But your body doesn't come with a built-in regulator for your emotions. It needs repeated early experiences with caregivers who help you regulate your distress and emotions—maybe hundreds and hundreds of times—to develop the skills needed to regulate your emotions.

Trauma survivors who never had the chance to develop these skills frequently find themselves dysregulated or out of sorts with regard to their bodies, moods, emotions, relationships, and lives in general. At these times, things often feel completely chaotic, and they are unable to take the actions needed to reestablish a sense of equilibrium. We talk a lot more about common post-traumatic self-regulation difficulties in chapter 2.

Systemic and Institutional Trauma

Outside the family system, there are organizations and other systems capable of inflicting similar harm and causing long-lasting pain. Religious institutions. The military. Organized sports. Schools. Corporations. We're hearing endless stories now of the vulnerability of people across many industries and organizations in which a code of silence protects those in power and people collude to

Starting at birth,
we are all wired for
attachment.

allow abuse to happen. And then, when it happens, there is a rush to cover it up. For various reasons (i.e., intimidation tactics), it is difficult to escape from these closed systems and scary, sometimes impossible, for victims to reach out for help.

Systemic or institutional racism is the same problem on a grand scale. It is defined as "the systemic distribution of resources, power, and opportunity in our society to the benefit of people who are white and the exclusion of people of color." Systemic racism is maintained by a broad range of institutional policies and practices that disadvantage specific ethnic and racial groups. Unfortunately, we can see evidence of this kind of racism everywhere we look: government surveillance, the criminal justice system, immigration arrests, infant mortality, stereotyped caricatures, and under- or distorted representations of racial or ethnic groups in the media or within institutions. As a consequence of systemic racism, racial disparities and stratification have occurred in health care, employment, housing, education, government, and other sectors.

The cumulative weight of these practices, along with repetitive experiences of bigotry and discrimination experienced directly and indirectly, has a serious, negative effect on the physical and mental health of Black, Indigenous, and People of Color. Race-based stress or trauma is often ongoing, pervasive, and generationally transmitted—beliefs, fears, and social identities are passed from one generation to the next. Racial trauma, in the form of both macroaggressions (overt racial or ethnic slurs, threats of harm or injury, shaming or humiliating interactions, experiencing or witnessing race-based brutality) and microaggressions (indirect, subtle, unintentional, or intentional slights) against people from these groups has huge cumulative effects on individuals and entire communities. Research suggests that people who experience racial trauma, particularly when layered on top of experiences associated with systemic racism, are vulnerable to developing PTSD or PTSD-like symptoms such as overall heightened anxiety, flashbacks, nightmares, poor self-concept, and depressed mood.

The effects of all kinds of racism, religious prejudice, stigma, sexism, homophobia, and xenophobia (to name only a few of the many possible societal offenses) are still inadequately recognized and addressed within society and within systems of mental health care. We in the psychotherapy field are guilty all too often of minimizing, missing, and ignoring the domain of social stigma and oppression. In taking clients' histories, therapists still commonly neglect to ask about experiences of racism and other forms of prejudice and discrimination in the same way that they might directly ask about exposure to violence or abuse. Even though I work hard to understand the experiences of my clients, I can't even begin to put myself in the shoes of a Black teenager growing up in a lower-income neighborhood within a predominantly white society, taking in messages about her worth and her future. I can't pretend to understand the experience of my client who was displaced as a young girl because of violence and war, and who came to the United States after a long period in a refugee camp only to face more racism and religious animosity. As a white therapist, I am committed to listening, asking questions, and making the implicit explicit in therapy sessions, offering opportunities to examine the emotional effects of racism and other forms of discrimination. The EMDR professional community is strongly committed to dismantling racism in our world and supporting cultural competence and sensitivity in our EMDR-trained clinicians.

The effects of
race-based trauma—
fears, beliefs, and
social identities—
are passed on from
one generation to the next.

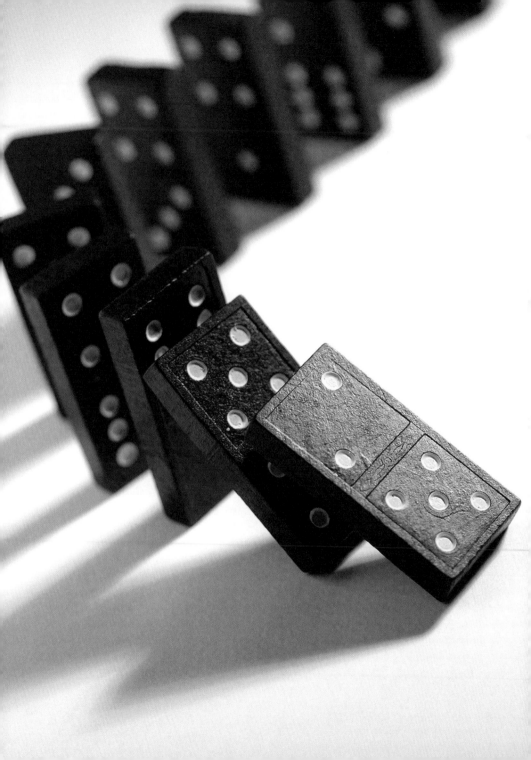

Michael was fortunate to grow up in a privileged environment, racially, ethnically, and economically. But even that could not protect him from trauma. And ironically, it's possible that Michael's privilege effectively kept his therapists from seeing the signs of his past abuse and neglect. Perhaps their cultural biases kept them from even asking critical questions. When I first met Michael, he shared with me that no therapist had ever inquired about trauma until he met Dr. Jeffrey Magnavita. Sadly, I have heard this same story all too often. He talked with his therapists about his phobias, his anxiety, his self-esteem issues, and his compensations for feeling insecure inside. On the surface, none of these difficulties suggested "trauma" per se. But taken collectively and viewed from above, it eventually became clear that they were the manifestations of an extensive history of trauma.

At the core of Michael's symptoms was a deep sense of insecurity, within himself and out in the world; he felt unmoored, unseen, and worthless. When bad things happened to him as a child, he felt like he had nowhere to go, nobody safe to turn to for help. He learned how to push these feelings as far away as possible and how to pretend in order to make it in the world while holding on to the precarious approval or acceptance of his parents. The phobias around heights and bridges and bathrooms and women and intimacy, the grandiosity, and the materialism were all clues to what lay beneath the surface for Michael and what would later be understood as attempts to keep everything painful and unbearable at bay. These attempts or self-protective maneuvers were just cloaks thrown over his core sense of defectiveness and mistrust—*I'm not good enough. I'm unlovable. I'm not safe in this world.* The avoidance and cloaks worked for a while—but the cost was enormous.

To effectively treat these symptoms, Michael had to dig deeper, to look for those missing pieces that would help him understand his symptoms within the context of a disturbing and lonely child-hood. And he would have to process his traumatic memories until he was free of their influence.

When there is no one
to trust or turn to,
we withdraw—even
from ourselves.

2

How Does Trauma Affect Your Mind, Body, and Behavior?

Michael: From my earliest days as a student into my adulthood, I was never able to read books and comprehend their plots or details. The words would flow past, but I was unable to get them to form a story. It was like I was looking at an impressionist painting but standing so close to it I couldn't see the whole picture. I saw the individual words, but they didn't create any overall meaning when strung together. "Reading Comprehension" was always my biggest downfall in any standardized testing.

Worse, I couldn't understand the lyrics or stories in songs—I would hear language, of course, but it didn't add up to anything I could hold in my mind. Friends in high school and college would be singing along or would shout, "Turn it up! I love this song!" Watching their joy and excitement made me feel essentially handicapped in some way I didn't quite understand. My experience at the few live concerts I went to with friends was always the same: I never knew the songs or the band members' names, and as I stood in the sea of people trying to sing along, I felt like an imposter—and a failure. Led Zeppelin, Fleetwood Mac, Steely Dan—my inability to "hear" their songs meant that I was somehow lacking in an important social currency, and that left me feeling even more isolated.

Then, when I needed to communicate, my handwriting was barely legible. I couldn't even read the notes I'd taken in class, or, later, in meetings. I would try to write as fast as my mind was going—imagine trying to finish eating while the waiter is taking away your plate—but would end up with half words and scribbles. At work, I couldn't type without constantly backspacing and correcting, leaving me stymied—I had *so many ideas*, but few ways to capture them for my clients or colleagues.

All of this made me feel like I couldn't take what I needed *in* and couldn't let what I wanted to express *out*. I was trapped.

Moreover, I was cut off. Even in therapy I would discuss the problems I was having but couldn't access any related emotions, no matter how we came at them. One therapist, frustrated by my inability, finally said to me, "Mr. Baldwin, you can sit there and pretend like you have no feelings about this, but you will die a lonely man." Ouch! That only made me feel more desperate and hopeless.

With every passing year his prediction seemed to be coming true. Yet feeling emotions other than fear just seemed to be one more thing I was incapable of. Between the anxiety attacks, nightmares, and regular phobic reactions, it felt like I was wearing out my body and brain with constant fear.

I thought of all these things as my defining characteristics, my quirks, my flaws, the immutable facts of who I was.

I eventually learned that I couldn't have been more wrong.

HOW TRAUMA EVENTUALLY CATCHES UP WITH US

Some people enter trauma treatment soon after a traumatic experience, within weeks or months. Many others come into treatment after being able to function "well enough" for many years, able to

Trauma handicaps our ability to adapt and adjust to our external world.

manage and move their lives along. Perhaps they were fortunate enough to have had some kind of anchor, like a healthy relationship or a rewarding job. But eventually, some challenge or transition—a loss, an illness, a move, a downsizing—tips their nervous system into a place where whatever had been running just below the surface starts to intrude. Those strategies that had kept emotions and memories in check stop working. When I respond to inquiries about treatment, I hear things like, "Lately, I can't sleep." "I can't eat." "I'm really short-tempered." "I just can't get out of bed." "I can't concentrate, and I'm worried that I'm going to get fired." "My husband pointed out that I'm washing my hands, like, a hundred times a day." "I'm just deeply unhappy." "I feel scared all the time." "I suddenly can't get my abusive father out of my mind."

It can even be something in the news that overloads or triggers their nervous system. My phone started ringing off the hook after 9/11. Even for people who hadn't been in New York or Washington, DC, and didn't know anyone who had died, the terrorist attacks quickly and, in some cases, unexpectedly, brought up feelings of danger, unpredictability, and evil, which stirred up childhood trauma memories they hadn't thought about in years or, in some cases, hadn't previously remembered. News reports about Harvey Weinstein, Michael Jackson, Jeffrey Epstein, Brett Kavanaugh, Bill Cosby, and those accused in the clergy abuse scandals regularly found their way into weekly therapy sessions, because they stirred up old feelings of helplessness and hopelessness, memories of not being believed, and the sense of impotence and invisibility that came when attempts were made to confront those in power.

The coronavirus pandemic is yet another big-T trauma that has affected us all. Research tells us that certain factors are likely to dramatically increase fear and perceptions of acute danger: when a threat is new and unfamiliar, when people believe they have little control over the threat, and when they experience a feeling of dread. The COVID-19 crisis contains all these key elements. For individuals with significant trauma histories or those who were already living in unsafe or unstable environments, the stress of the pandemic was the straw that broke the camel's back. The sense of vulnerability, uncertainty, and terror that marked the early months of the pandemic triggered memories of previous adversity, loss, and, for some, life-threatening encounters. For the client who was a POW in Vietnam and for the survivor of domestic violence, the stay-at-home orders activated memories of captivity and powerlessness, as well as childhood memories of isolation and loneliness. For others, reading about COVID-19 patients who had died alone, without their families, brought up unresolved feelings of grief and, at times, guilt about the loss of friends and family members to overdoses, suicide, and illness. The loss of jobs and financial security during this period has created tremendous anxiety for people and has reactivated memories of times when the rug was unexpectedly pulled out from under their feet.

Census Bureau data collected during the early months of the pandemic indicated that more than a third of all Americans were showing signs of clinical depression or anxiety or both. These findings represent a huge escalation from before the pandemic. For example, before the pandemic, 25 percent of US adults reported having a depressed mood, but in the midst of the pandemic, around July 2020, 50 percent—double the number of people—reported experiencing a depressed mood.

It's also not uncommon for survivors to become symptomatic and reach out for help when a perpetrator dies; suddenly, it's safe to remember, feel, or speak. Or perhaps they start to recall what happened to them, finding themselves unable to "hold it together" once their own child turns the age that they were when abused. Many come to recognize that there has been a little-kid voice inside all along, saying, "I can't speak up. I won't be believed. I'll just be punished. I have to stay very still and not make waves." Even though, as an adult, they know their perpetrator is now ninety years old, living a thousand miles away in a nursing home, deceased, or in jail, these kinds of thoughts, coupled with an unrelenting sense of fear, keep them from knowing their own story.

One of the first steps in treatment is exploration, because it's not unusual to discover that clients have no idea why they are suddenly in trouble psychologically or why they are choosing to finally pursue therapy after suffering for such a long time. Out of this abyss, we start to get a foothold and begin to chart a course for healing. As we move into discussing the effects of trauma, particularly chronic trauma, on day-to-day functioning, it's helpful first to discuss two relevant frameworks: the Window of Tolerance and the Change Triangle.

The Window of Tolerance

The Window of Tolerance, a concept first articulated by psychiatrist Daniel Siegel in 1999 (and later expanded by others; see notes), is offered here as a frame of reference to help you better understand your symptoms and their relationship to activation or arousal within your nervous system. Think about this window as you study and get to know your own body's reactions to internal (feelings and physical sensations) as well as external (perceived threat) stimuli.

The Window of Tolerance

Hyper-arousal Zone	Overreactive. Overwhelmed. Emotionally distressed. Can't calm down. Racing thoughts.
Window of Tolerance (Optimal Arousal Zone)	Able to think clearly. Connected to body and emotions. Fully present.
Hypo-arousal Zone	Depressed. Lethargic. Numb. Shut down. Absence of emotion and sensation. Impaired cognitive processing.

People with trauma in their histories tend to get stuck in patterns of hyper-arousal—"too much" activation, high anxiety, ruminative worry, and distress—or hypo-arousal—"too little" activation that involves shutting down, numbing, or suppressing feelings in an attempt to dampen the jumpiness in their nervous systems. When my clients present in a state of hyper-arousal, I observe extreme restlessness, signs of panic, trembling, pressured speech and actions, a readiness to flee, stressed breathing, and immobilized but agitated behavior. I hear complaints like, "I'm so overwhelmed," "I can't bear this," "I can't relax." Hypo-arousal represents the other end of the spectrum. When clients present in this state, there may be little observable movement or emotion and they appear zoned out, far away, or inwardly focused. Clients will often comment, "I can't think or focus," "I'm numb and can't feel anything," or "I feel shut down and disconnected." Many trauma survivors find themselves fluctuating between the two states, tamping down distress as long as they can—barely living, only existing—until the next trigger comes along, and suddenly, they're flooded with panic, intrusive memories, and the impulse to escape from the fright or the emotional pain.

In this chapter and those that follow, we talk about the importance of learning how to increase your tolerance of intense internal states, both on your own and with the help of others, particularly a therapist. The goal is to learn how to modulate the temperature on your emotional thermostat to feel more in control and able to think straight, function at your best, and engage in the work of recovery. Ideally, you want to be in the optimal arousal zone with an ever-expanding window of tolerance. When you are able to expand and stay within this window, you're able to connect with your memories, feelings, and physical body. You are able to be fully present, emotionally, and can attend to your moment-to-moment experience without shutting down or getting overwhelmed. You are able to coherently describe and reflect on your internal experience. Here, within this well-regulated corridor, you can be fully alive, curious about yourself and others, playful, flexible, and confident in your ability to make meaning out of what you are observing, both internally and out in the world.

Michael lived in a state of chronic hypo-arousal. To use his words, he was "numb and disconnected from feelings and memories, aloof and distant from others, and obsessed with appearances." He felt little in terms of genuine emotion. His workaholism, dissociation, drinking, spending, avoidance of intimacy, preoccupation with status, and maintenance of grandiosity were all in the service of regulating fear and anxiety and keeping a lid on his traumatic memories and relational pain. Most of the time, that plan worked, but every now and then, when he was approached by a woman seeking romance, when he had to cross a bridge, or when he felt rejected or close to failure, he would get panicky and feel compelled to run. He would get thrown into a state of hyper-arousal and have to bear down even harder to try to push the terror and despair away. It was a vicious cycle that took him deeper and deeper into self-sabotaging behaviors.

The Change Triangle

As Hilary Jacobs Hendel writes in her book *It's Not Always Depression*, "The Change Triangle is a map of the mind . . . No matter what is upsetting you, what symptoms of stress you are suffering from, what unwanted behaviors you have, or what aspects of your personality you want to change, the Change Triangle provides a logical, science-based path to relief and recovery." Ideally, along with all the other information we're offering you here, learning a little about the Change Triangle will give you a useful lens through which to view yourself and your struggles. I trust that it will serve to increase your readiness for EMDR therapy.

The Change Triangle®

DEFENSES
Anything we
do to avoid
feeling

INHIBITORY EMOTIONS
Anxiety,
Shame, Guilt

CORE EMOTIONS
Fear, Anger, Sadness, Disgust, Joy,
Excitement, Sexual Excitement

OPEN-HEARTED STATE of the AUTHENTIC SELF
Calm, Curious, Connected, Compassionate,
Confident, Courageous, Clear

The three corners of the triangle are labeled "Core Emotions," "Inhibitory Emotions," and "Defenses." Core emotions include sadness or grief, anger, joy, fear, excitement, including sexual excitement, and disgust. Each of these emotions, hardwired in our brains from birth and connected to a range of impulses that ensure survival, help us know what we want and like (or don't) and then, what we need to do. When we make room for our core emotions and their associated impulses, always experienced physically in our bodies, and allow ourselves to fully feel and process them, we are on our way to freeing ourselves from symptoms and distress and empowering ourselves to triumphantly forge ahead.

However, if back in time you learned to inhibit those core emotions for fear of negative consequences, you'll likely experience some degree of anxiety, shame, or guilt when those emotions emerge, even when they barely break into consciousness. Often, with little awareness, you'll find yourself hitting the brakes on those core emotions. Inhibitory emotions, in the upper right corner of the triangle, signal "Danger," "Stop"; you start shutting down instantaneously, without even thinking. As a result of that radical shutdown, you might find yourself feeling seriously uncomfortable in your body—distressed breathing, tightness in your muscles, an unbearable sense of pressure. Perhaps, you experience an urge to get away from that discomfort in any way possible, physically or psychologically.

Unbearable core emotions trigger not only inhibitory emotions but also defensive reactions and patterns. Defenses, in the upper left corner, are any actions meant to help us avoid painful emotions and distress. Some softer defenses can be helpful and even necessary for short-term coping (humor, distraction, changing the subject in order to stay focused), but most defenses, when used regularly to ward off emotions, pain, or anxiety, leave us rigidly locked into unhealthy patterns and detached from our true selves.

Sometimes people defend against particular emotions with other emotions, like my client Jim, whose wife died, triggering memories of losing his mother and brother at a very young age in a car accident. At the start of treatment, he pushed away his grief and tears with bouts of rage and self-hatred and refused to consider that his response was also about the loss of his mother and brother. Once he was able to acknowledge those primary losses and the accompanying traumas in childhood, his rage dissipated, and he was able to feel—and heal—his grief.

As we look more closely at trauma-related symptoms, keep the window of tolerance and the Change Triangle in mind. Think about where your symptoms are on these maps and what that might mean for you—both in general and as you respond moment to moment to the world around you. The greater your awareness of your emotions and defenses, and the more you are aware of how they might connect to earlier adverse life experiences, the more effectively you will be able to use therapy.

In therapy, you'll work to expand your window of tolerance, increasing your ability to safely access, regulate, and process emotion. When you are able to live in this optimal zone, connected to yourself and to others, living and loving fully, you will be at your best. Hard to imagine? Well, even if you can't make much sense out of things right now, hang in there. Help is around the corner.

FORMAL DIAGNOSES

The long-term adverse consequences of trauma exposure remain hard to define and categorize. And making a diagnosis is a

Emotional self-regulation
is the ability to modulate
your own emotional
thermostat.

complicated process. No two people have the same set of symptoms, and many of the trauma survivors I see in treatment actually meet the criteria for *many* different diagnoses—mood disorders, anxiety disorders, eating disorders, addictive disorders, attention deficit hyperactivity disorder, and personality disorders such as borderline personality disorder or obsessive compulsive personality disorder—in addition to meeting the criteria for disorders explicitly defined as trauma-related syndromes—PTSD, complex PTSD (C-PTSD), and various dissociative disorders. For some, a diagnosis feels validating, explanatory, and helpful. ("Wow, I'm not the only one! There is actually a name for this.") For others, it may seem like yet another negative label that feels shameful or burdensome.

In this section, for the most part, we only briefly and intermittently mention formal diagnoses or "disorders." Instead, we offer you an overview of the kinds of symptoms, patterns, and difficulties most commonly associated with a history of childhood and/or adult trauma. It is helpful for my clients to understand their symptoms as related to both big-*T* and little-*t* experiences. As we look at their suffering through a trauma lens, we are able to embrace their story with compassion and create an EMDR plan that offers them hope, clear recovery steps, and a promise of relief and emotional healing.

TRAUMA-BASED SYMPTOMS

Three primary and universally recognized kinds of symptoms come into play with trauma: intrusive symptoms, avoidant symptoms, and hyper-arousal symptoms. This cluster of symptoms is most commonly associated with the diagnosis of post-traumatic stress disorder (PTSD).

Intrusive Symptoms — *Reexperiencing Traumatic Events*

Intrusive symptoms can be painfully debilitating and are often the ones that bring clients into treatment. These symptoms are related to the reexperiencing of traumatic events or, perhaps, aspects of events; one might reexperience them as intrusive images or sensory experiences (the car careening out of control, the smell of smoke), thoughts (*I'm going to die!*), bodily sensations (heart racing, sweating, pain), or debilitating emotions (fear, shame). Other examples are distressing dreams and nightmares related in some way to real-life traumas. Sometimes, even behaviors associated with traumatic encounters—running away, hiding, freezing, or fighting—can get triggered and reenacted. Understandably, people can feel like they're losing their minds when they experience "flashbacks"—smelling, hearing, seeing, or experiencing something that isn't actually there or actually happening. People are moving through their day and then suddenly, they are five years old again, feeling like they are reliving the experience of being at the family dinner table with a raging parent. They are in Afghanistan. They are in their car as it tumbles end over end. It's a disorienting experience; without notice, they lose their grounding and orientation to the present moment, and suddenly the past collides with the present.

Frequently, it happens at the most inopportune of times—while giving a presentation, driving, parenting, or having sex. It's the ultimate sense of powerlessness when people feel like they are at the mercy of their memories. And, of course, their world then starts to shrink as they try to avoid the people, places, and things that trigger those intrusions.

When people have worked hard to push their trauma out of conscious awareness, as was the case with Michael, intrusive symptoms feel particularly frightening and disabling because when they strike, there's often absolutely no context. In the mental health field, it is now commonly accepted that the brain is, indeed, capable of "holding back" memories it deems too potentially debilitating to remember. For many years now, a vast body of research evidence has been showing that it is *not rare at all* for people who were sexually abused in childhood to go for many years, even decades, without having any recognizable or obvious memories of that abuse.

When people who don't consciously recall what happened to them are suddenly seized with terror, nausea, flashes of images, or, like Michael, nightmares, recurring over and over with no idea what they might mean, it can be crazy making. Some clients have even asked me whether I think they are possessed. "No," I tell them, "it's just your brain letting you know that there's something important that you need to attend to—something that needs to be properly processed and resolved. We'll definitely be addressing this together."

Avoidant Symptoms — *Steering Clear of What Makes Us Anxious*

When we encounter people, places, and circumstances that make us anxious, we tend to avoid them. It makes sense, right? The anxiety serves as a clue, telling us that we are in some amount of danger. And we evolved to avoid danger. But for trauma survivors, it is difficult to know if the avoidance is adaptive or, in fact, misinformed. The urge to run from or avoid might be a fragment of an earlier memory continuing to exert its influence in the present when there actually is no danger at all.

If the original danger was present when we weren't old enough to be *able* to avoid it, the only choice left to us was to shut down, pull away, or dissociate—to mentally leave if we couldn't physically leave. The problem comes when these coping mechanisms—disconnecting, numbing out, or fleeing to avoid potential harm—carry over into adulthood and we wind up closing ourselves off from intimacy, joy, and openhearted connection to the world around us. We cease to live and love in a meaningful way and no longer know what it means to be fully alive. And here's the thing: It's never a permanent solution. We can't avoid everything all the time, and sooner or later something always breaks through that barrier.

Hyper-Arousal Symptoms — *Endlessly on High Alert*

Hyper-arousal symptoms reflect the body's need to remain hyper-vigilant for fear that danger lurks right around the next corner. It's the sense of always being on edge, hyper-reactive to sounds or smells or another person's tone of voice. Often people in this state startle easily and find it difficult to sleep, rest, and concentrate. Because their internal alarm system is stuck in high gear, they may seem impulsive, reckless, or prone to self-destructive behavior. In relationships, they never feel a sense of true safety or have the ability to relax and enjoy what is being offered in the present moment. The hyper-vigilant person exists in a state of anticipatory anxiety, waiting to be criticized, hurt, abused, or abandoned.

Without treatment, many people remain at the mercy of that panic and agitation or find ways to numb out, avoid, or self-medicate. We'll discuss this in more detail later in the chapter.

When exposure to trauma is prolonged, chronic, and interpersonal in nature—such as with childhood abuse and neglect, or ongoing domestic violence—the symptom picture is typically even more complex. In addition to the symptoms described above,

Trauma survivors adopt a range of strategies to keep from remembering, knowing, and feeling:

Grandiosity

People-pleasing

Caretaking

Workaholism

Perfectionism

Deflection

Misdirected anger

Over-responsibility

Apologizing

Self-criticism

Picking fights

Blaming self or others

Risk taking

Promiscuity

Addictive/compulsive behaviors

Gambling

Sex/pornography

Alcohol and drugs

Overeating

Anorexia/bulimia

Self-injury

Suicidal thinking

Lying

Obsessive thinking

Talking nonstop

Intellectualizing

Changing the subject

Numbing
Dissociating
Disengaging
Refusal to accept
what is
Refusal to grieve
Avoidance
Withdrawal
Isolation
Detaching/not caring
Fatigue
Laughing and joking
Fogginess
Self-hatred

Externalizing
Minimizing
Sarcasm
Pushing others away
Arrogance/entitlement
Aggression
Attacking or judging others
Dismissive attitude
Rationalizing
Overactivity
Excessive sleeping
Denial
Procrastination
Controlling behavior

people who have endured repeated traumas over extended periods of time may develop symptoms associated with a diagnosis of complex post-traumatic stress disorder, or C-PTSD.

WHEN WE ARE AT THE MERCY OF OUR EMOTIONS —
Emotional Dysregulation

Much of what I do in therapy is about helping people access and process emotions that they weren't able—or allowed—to feel and express earlier in life because of family norms, limited coping skills, or the lack of safety and healthy supports. When a child grows up in an environment where feelings are viewed negatively and he gets punished, ignored, or mocked for expressing them, that child learns to disengage from emotion. He never learns how to constructively handle emotions, so they wind up being experienced as overwhelming and disabling, dangerous, and intolerable.

Overt manifestations of emotonal dysregulation might include angry outbursts and violent behavior toward others, uncontrollable crying, despair, and withdrawal, or a total bodily collapse. Many survivors develop a serious fear of emotions; because they can potentially render you helpless and unable to function, they must be avoided at all costs. Survivors typically live at the top of the Change Triangle—phobic of their core emotions—with a window of tolerance that is often quite narrow. The negative emotions that regularly burden my clients include fear, sadness or grief, anger at self and others, guilt, and shame. They also struggle with states of unbearable aloneness and heartbreak. And interestingly, even though emotional dysregulation typically refers to difficulties in dealing with negative emotions, sometimes positive emotions are experienced as equally overwhelming and threatening. They've learned that positive feelings can seduce you into lowering your guard and can set you up for rejection and disappointment. Examples of positive emotions and states often associated with anxiety and discomfort include pride, joy and enjoyment, excitement and sexual attraction or desire, love and longing, and hope.

WHEN WE NEED TO TAKE ACTION TO WARD OFF PAIN —
Behavioral Dysregulation

Many behavioral symptoms are about avoidance or defense—protecting *against* or distracting *from* traumatic memories and unbearable emotions. When they are feeling overwhelmed and unable to bear their pain, people reach for behavioral strategies to regulate emotional distress so they can work, take care of their kids, and maintain some semblance of sanity. Behavioral dysregulation refers to the self-protective things that people *do* to try to manage emotional dysregulation. Here, we're at the top left side of the Change Triangle, where we might observe a range of defensive actions with the primary goal of avoiding intolerable emotions. One of my clients, a recovering alcoholic who recently completed EMDR therapy, now recognizes the connection between certain emotions and his lifelong pattern of binge drinking. "My father would call me names and tell me that I was weak and pathetic if I'd get tearful or emotional, even for a millisecond. By the time I was in my teens, I was already an alcoholic. When I'd feel sad, I'd feel ashamed, and when I'd feel ashamed, I'd reach for a drink. My father would also accuse me of being naïve and gullible if I dared to express excitement about anything. As a result, I wouldn't let myself get excited. I'd start to look forward to something and I'd shut it down. I'd drink and quickly forget that I was ever excited."

Symptoms and
survival strategies
are often a reflection
of underlying trauma.

Shame (*I'm a pathetic, terrible person*) is often a central emotional experience for survivors, and they will go to great lengths, consciously or unconsciously, to avoid having it triggered. They are unwilling to risk making another "mistake." A "mistake" like trusting too much, wanting too much, or feeling too much. A "mistake" like being too assertive or too submissive. A "mistake" like sharing too much, expressing anger, or showing vulnerability with the wrong people. A "mistake" like daring to hope that things could be better or redemption could be possible.

People sometimes attempt to cope with emotional pain by engaging in self-injury, such as banging their heads, cutting, burning, scratching, or forcefully punching themselves. Of course, there can be many different functions associated with these behaviors (for example, self-punishment, expression of feelings, attempts to numb oneself or feel some relief or release, externalization of the pain inside, a cry for help), but more often than not, it's about engaging in an action that keeps one from being overwhelmed by emotional distress. It's a desperate but reliable way to avoid the worst emotional pain.

Addictive and compulsive behaviors can also serve as a way to numb out or escape from the pain—drugs, alcohol, pornography, gambling, spending, sex, food, workaholism. Unfortunately, when people have not processed or resolved the trauma or pain that underlies the addictive or compulsive behavior, they get one addiction under control and, before they know it, find themselves resorting to other addictive behaviors in an attempt to better tolerate or avoid the explosive memories and feelings inside.

When Michael started treatment with Dr. Magnavita, he was addicted to his grandiose lifestyle. He medicated himself with alcohol and Vicodin and defended against his sense of worthlessness and insecurity by buying the biggest and the best and the most. And, of course, he relied on his workaholism, our most socially acceptable addiction, to make it through each day. Only after he was well into his recovery did he come to understand that these behaviors represented a desperate, ongoing attempt to manage a state of extreme emotional dysregulation.

WHEN WE DON'T TRUST KEY RELATIONSHIPS —
Relational Dysregulation

Because children are so dependent on others and can't make it in the world by themselves, they do what they have to do to ensure that they don't lose or alienate or disappoint important "attachment figures." Abused children often work to become everything they think their parent or caregiver wants them to be. They swallow their feelings, complaints, and pain and remain silent, sometimes even becoming their parent's little assistant and working to keep the peace in their household or family.

What this means for their relationships later in life is that they come to believe that they can't count on nurturance, warmth, or support from anyone. As a result, they become guarded and mistrustful in relationships, always waiting for the other shoe to drop, always waiting to be abandoned or shamed or abused or accused of lying. Relationships then become fraught with triggers that can lead to conflict, rageful outbursts, or abrupt ruptures; collapse or paralysis; and even depression and suicidality if the pain is inescapable and too difficult to bear.

Some grow up to present themselves as having no needs in relationships. They give up on expecting anything, accepting whatever they get, and holding their cards close to their chest. Or they

Even if you get one addiction under control—without processing your trauma, you may soon be in the grip of another.

may go to the other extreme, becoming very demanding and entitled: "I never got it back then, so you better give it to me now." For many, relationships are confusing and chaotic.

For Michael, it was "attachment at any cost." He was willing to sacrifice everything to maintain his connection to his parents, trying to obtain their love. He learned how to be a perfect little boy. This ability to adapt and read the needs of others became an invaluable part of Michael's coping skill set. He learned how to look good and sound good and be gracious with people, and that no doubt served him well professionally. But Michael's willingness to do just about anything to obtain and maintain connection led to situations as an adult in which he was taken advantage of.

This concept of *attachment at any cost* is also relevant in the context of the #MeToo movement. We have heard accounts of women and men who did what they felt they had to do to maintain their safety, their livelihoods, and their complicated relationships; many knew that they couldn't bite the hand that fed them. When you feel powerless within a system, you do what you need to do to survive. You learn to forget. Perhaps, you block things out; your mind goes to work on your behalf to help you carry on.

It might be important to mention here that people with fears or anxieties around intimacy often assume that they must have been sexually abused as children. That is not necessarily the case. It could be that they were physically or emotionally abused and, as a result, can't tolerate vulnerability. Or, perhaps, they came from a neglectful environment in which they had to shut down any and all longing or desire, since it wasn't safe to have needs. To engage intimately, you have to be able to attune to your body, slow down, and relax. For many trauma survivors, that just doesn't seem safe or possible, and so attempts at intimacy often fail.

WHEN OUR BODIES REACT TO TRAUMA —
Somatic Dysregulation

We know that elevated stress hormone levels contribute to many physical ailments, so it makes sense that clients frequently arrive in my office with a variety of medical or physical problems, like irritable bowel syndrome, panic attacks, asthma, migraines, headaches, chronic fatigue and fibromyalgia, chemical sensitivities, pain, and other stress-related illnesses. These kinds of physical symptoms or syndromes are often highly correlated with a history of trauma.

In the Adverse Childhood Experiences Study (ACE Study), conducted by Kaiser Permanente and the Centers for Disease Control and Prevention, adverse childhood experiences were found to be highly predictive of health and psychological problems across the life span. Researchers found that maltreatment (emotional, physical, and sexual abuse and/or neglect) and household dysfunction in childhood contribute to health problems that manifest decades later, including chronic diseases such as cancer, stroke, heart disease, and diabetes—some of the most prominent causes of death and disability in our country. Ten types of childhood trauma were identified in the study; each type, if present in someone's history, was given a score of one. So a person's ACE score might range from zero to ten. For example, if you were abandoned by your father as a young child, raised by an alcoholic mother, and sexually abused by a teacher at school, you would have an ACE score of three. The findings suggest that the higher the number of adverse childhood experiences (ACE), the higher the number of medical symptoms and addictions. As described by the noted psychiatrist Bessel van der Kolk in his outstanding *New York Times* bestseller, *The Body Keeps the Score*, the consequences of adverse life experiences can

Trauma can affect
all vital body systems:

nervous

cardiac

circulatory

respiratory

digestive

endocrine

excretory

immune

reproductive

skeletal

muscular

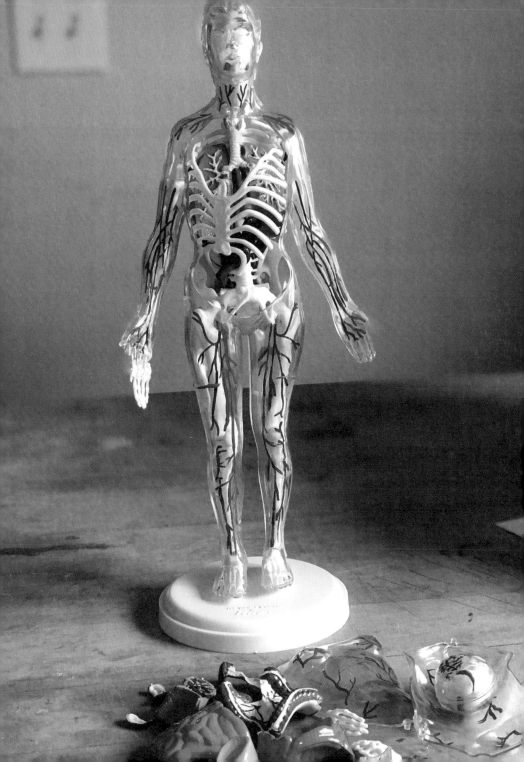

be seen years later in somatically based symptoms and bodily ailments. Compared with an ACE score of zero (no exposure to adverse childhood events), having an ACE score of four was associated with two times the risk of receiving a diagnosis of cancer, a fourfold increase in emphysema, and a sevenfold (700 percent) increase in alcoholism. Taking us back to our discussion of emotional dysregulation and survivors' desperate attempts to manage psychological pain, it is worth noting that an ACE score above six correlated with a thirtyfold (3,000 percent) increase in attempted suicides.

The ten-item questionnaire from the ACE Study can be found in our Appendix.

WHEN WE CREATE MENTAL ESCAPE ROUTES —
Attentional Dysregulation and Dissociation

We all have the ability to intentionally filter out information in our surroundings. This ability enables us to focus, read a book in a café, or take a phone call on the street. For those with a significant trauma history, applying these filters can be next to impossible. Trauma survivors often feel chronically overstimulated, finding it hard to concentrate on what's important. Left untreated, their difficulties often persist for years or even decades, as seen in Michael's lifelong struggles with tasks that demanded focused attention, like reading and learning words to songs. His frequent falls leading to multiple concussions also may have been an indication of his attentional dysregulation and tendency to regularly disconnect from the world around him.

Furthermore, when individuals, especially children, are faced with extreme threats or circumstances that feel impossible to bear, the brain does this filtering by itself, spontaneously blocking out from conscious awareness what it perceives as intolerable. This is dissociation.

We can think of dissociation as the act of fleeing psychologically when physical escape is not possible. It happens automatically; there is no contemplation, no choice, no decision to be made. It is about psychological survival in the moment.

A traumatized child relies on this protective mechanism to block out or separate from overwhelming and intolerable experiences. Dissociation in childhood is associated with states of freeze (a high level of distress coupled with the inability to move—the proverbial deer in the headlights) and partial or complete mental and physical shutdown—a state of feigned death (complete submission or collapse—the possum that plays dead to survive a predator).

However, as the frequency and intensity of dissociative responses increases, this mechanism becomes counterproductive. My client Cindy, whose father regularly beat her mother in front of her and her siblings, used to "go away" the moment her father started to raise his voice. "I didn't choose to go away," she explained. "It would just happen. Tucked away behind a chair or the couch, I'd get very small, very foggy, and time would stand still. Everything would become very distant, and nothing felt real. I'd stop hearing my mother's screaming. I'd 'disappear' myself. After those episodes, I would feel so guilty that I didn't do something more to help my mother.

"As I got older, I would find myself spacing out in response to situations that were not actually threatening, just heated or emotionally intense. I became allergic to anger and other negative emotions. I'd freeze and 'go away' if I heard even a hint of anger in another person's voice—a friend, family member, or teacher. Dissociation became my default setting, and when my threat meter

When it's not possible
to physically escape harm,
we protect ourselves
by disappearing
psychologically.

spiked, I couldn't stick around. . . . I was gone." More recently, Cindy told me, "I want to learn how to remain present in the face of conflict and strong emotion. Dissociation may have saved my life, but now it is keeping me from being fully engaged in my life and in my most important relationships."

It's helpful to think about normal alterations in attention and consciousness and the signs of more significant dissociation as being on a continuum.

The Dissociative Continuum

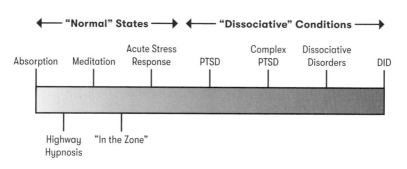

On the far-left side of our continuum, we have adaptive, healthy altered states of attention and consciousness, like getting absorbed in a TV show or book and not hearing what's going on in the next room, dropping into a meditative state, or "getting into the zone" during a sports competition or performance. Or highway hypnosis, where you pass exits two, three, and four but actually have no memory of them because you were listening to the car radio.

Moving along the continuum, we begin to see dissociative responses associated with acute stress and various trauma-related disorders, responses such as fogginess or spaciness, an inability to access feelings or talk about experiences, numbing out and disconnecting from one's body. *Depersonalization* is the term used to describe the sense of looking in at yourself from the outside and feeling as if you are in a dream. *Derealization* is the term used to describe the sense of wandering through a world that feels unreal and far away; there is a disconnection from one's surroundings, even a sense of disinterest.

As we travel toward the right end of the continuum, we move from PTSD and complex PTSD with some dissociative features to the dissociative disorders. With increased exposure to trauma (intensity, frequency, and duration), the need and tendency to dissociate increases. Ultimately, this can lead to a well-established division between the parts of a person that function in daily life and the parts that hold the components of the traumatic memories. Here, parts of the personality are often more fully developed, each with some sense of identity and a constellation of feelings, thoughts, and trauma-based reactions.

It helps to think about personality as a great big house, with screen doors between its different rooms, which are like the various parts of our personalities. Each part is associated with different aspects of our identity, our moods, our talents, our vulnerabilities. Perhaps there's the professional self, the parent self, and the playful self. These are parts that help us handle the tasks and challenges of everyday life as we shift from one role to the next as needed. And then, there are the traumatized parts, each carrying some aspect of the traumas experienced over the course of our lifetimes. Many of these are wounded-child parts, carrying trauma-based beliefs, feelings, and action impulses or reactions associated with threat or survival. That is, a young traumatized part may believe "I'm not safe in the world" and carry a sense of dread and anxiety with an impulse to flee or hide or collapse if there is a perceived threat.

Children learn to hide
the parts of themselves
that are not tolerated by
their caregivers.

Another part may carry the impulse to fight back. Another might respond to the perception of danger by searching for or clinging to a protective other. And yet another may choose to appease or give in to a person experienced as threatening—a strategy undoubtedly learned under dire early circumstances. At some level we can all identify with the concept of parts of our personality, but the further along the continuum we are, the thicker the walls and doors between the different parts of the personality become.

At the far-right end of the continuum, we see the most complex manifestation of dissociation—dissociative identity disorder (DID), formerly known as multiple personality disorder. With DID, there are thick walls and doors between the rooms of the house, between the different parts of the personality. When one distinct identity takes control of the person's behavior, it can lead to "blank spells" or "time loss." There is literally amnesia for certain encounters, where one part of a person is not aware of the activities of another part; certain experiences, internal and/or external, are simply not available to other parts.

A child may have one part that goes to school and another part that deals with an abusive father at night. An adult may have one part that functions at work and another that hides in the closet when it gets dark outside, reliving the abuses of childhood with no orientation to time or place. People with DID sometimes hear voices inside their heads and report that other people describe things that they have said or done that they do not remember and that seem out of character for them. It is critical for individuals with symptoms associated with the far-right side of the continuum to seek treatment with a therapist specifically trained in treating dissociative disorders. This is a distinct specialty among trauma-informed and EMDR therapists.

WHEN WE FEEL BAD, PATHETIC, AND WEAK —
Negative Self-Concept

When children are hurt by someone who they depend on for survival, it may feel unsafe to show anger toward them. Instead, children often turn the anger toward a much safer target: themselves. Adults do the same. "He's a good man, he's a respected professional; it must be something about me. I'm bad, pathetic, weak, disgusting." They accept and internalize criticism and verbal abuse as if it represented the absolute truth.

This inclination toward self-blame and self-hatred, and the debilitating guilt, shame, and depressed mood that result, are typically related to a pervasive sense of confusion about issues related to responsibility. In fact, the phrase that I probably hear more than any other in my office is "I feel like it was my fault." A big piece of the work that I do with my clients involves challenging the framework that starts with "If only . . ." *If only* I had been a better girl, had done better in school, wasn't such a disappointment, hadn't been so needy, had remained quiet, had fought back, had protected my little brother better. Survivors often lack self-compassion, and struggle to see themselves as capable of self-acceptance, loving others, or receiving love.

From the start of therapy, we try to make room for a new perspective: *I did not deserve any of what happened to me. It wasn't my fault. I'm good, lovable, and strong.*

WHEN WE FEEL DIFFERENT — Isolation, Profound Aloneness, and
Sense of Alienation

People with significant trauma in their histories often feel intensely alone even in a crowd; they learned long ago that it wasn't safe to

When you blame yourself,
you can't move beyond
a sense of defectiveness
and despair.

(It wasn't your fault.)

share their true selves or genuine feelings. Even when people are successful and manage to engage with lots of people and activities in various work and social settings, as in Michael's case, they still have a sense of being different, not good enough, and painfully isolated.

Before his connection with Dr. Magnavita, Michael had never felt seen, understood, or truly known by anyone in his life. He had never shared his vulnerabilities, fears, or self-doubt with another human being. He was alienated from others *and* alienated from himself. He had never felt safe enough or supported enough to turn his attention inward, to begin the process of reengaging with the "exiled" parts of himself that carried the memories of childhood abuse and neglect. It was Dr. Magnavita's genuine interest, compassionate stance, and clarity in identifying the importance of the trauma in Michael's early life that helped him begin to emerge from his isolation and self-alienation. He sensed that Dr. Magnavita really wanted to know about his experiences, both as an adult and during his childhood; his warmth and curiosity gave Michael the courage to begin to look inside, to learn what was behind those closed doors, and to share what he found.

WHEN WE ABANDON ALL HOPE — *Loss of Purpose and Failure to Initiate*

When your basic frame of reference and core beliefs—*good people deserve to be treated well; children should be loved and protected; priests are supposed to take care of us and protect our families*—get shattered, again and again, often the only alternative left is to stop believing in anyone or anything and to shut down feelings and overall engagement with the world. Many trauma survivors learned as children not to hope or try, because expectations and dreams mean you've got farther to fall when you don't get what you're longing for or achieve what you're trying to achieve. While explaining to me why he couldn't even contemplate applying to college, my nineteen-year-old Latino client, son of non-English-speaking immigrants, shouted, "Who has time or energy to dream? I'm in survival mode, just trying to stay alive. And besides, I don't think I'd get in. I can't stand more disappointment."

For clients living in poverty and/or in communities with gun violence or high substance abuse mortality rates, there's this sense of having a foreshortened future—things are not going to get better and nobody's ever going to really understand or offer a way out. When you're trapped in an abusive or dysfunctional family, you learn that it is better to maintain the status quo than to aim for something better or different.

WHEN WE FAIL TO ATTEND TO OURSELVES — *Poor Self-Care*

Trauma survivors may not take good care of themselves for a number of reasons. My clients, particularly sexual abuse survivors, tend to avoid doctors and dentists, because going to an appointment can be overwhelming, triggering fear and an old feeling of being powerless and trapped. Needing a dentist to work on your teeth or a doctor to examine your body can activate shame, intense vulnerability, and other intrusive PTSD symptoms.

Dysregulated eating and sleeping habits are also a hallmark of trauma. Growing up, perhaps there were not many good role models to show what taking care of oneself or others looked like. Many learn to use food to soothe anxiety and sleep as an escape from depression and misery. Nighttime was often when bad things happened, so the idea of going to bed at night remains unsettling for many survivors all the way into adulthood. Also, it is not uncommon to find that people avoid bedtime because of nightmares or bad dreams. Sometimes drugs and alcohol become solutions, the only way to settle the body enough to entertain the possibility of sleep.

Those who learned to rely on dissociation as a primary coping strategy may find that their bodies feel foreign and unknown; there is no longer a relationship to or with one's physical self. The disconnect or depersonalization happened long ago, and now their bodies serve only as reminders of past traumas and failures to protect themselves. This disconnect and need to avoid can understandably lead to self-neglect. Some survivors can't look at themselves in a mirror and avoid going shopping for clothing. Some avoid exercise. Others ignore critical signs of illness in their bodies. Sadly, many end up dwelling in a place of self-hatred or body-hatred and come to believe *My body is shameful and unreliable.*

WHEN WE CAN'T SAY NO — *Poor Boundaries and Limit Setting*

Children need to be taught and shown that they are worthy of protection and entitled to have personal boundaries. The simple preschool phrase "Each of you needs to keep your hands to yourself" is an example of an early message about boundaries. Effective adult intervention when there is emotional or physical aggression between siblings or bullying by kids at school or in the neighborhood conveys the message that boundaries need to be respected and safety protected. When a child learns that their personal space can be violated, or that their feelings or needs don't matter, they don't learn to set limits or say no. As adults, they often wind up in relationships—in the workplace, community, or home—with people who don't respect their emotional or physical boundaries. They inadvertently choose people—controlling, invalidating, mis-attuned, or abusive—who continue to violate their boundaries in ways similar to how they were violated growing up.

Some clients are surprised to discover that they themselves need to have better boundaries with regard to their own behavior and ultimately must learn how to express their wants in less intrusive, more productive ways. As one client shared, "Since I was young, people would tell me to manage my impulses and use my words rather than simply taking what I wanted or demanding that my needs be immediately met. They thought that I had attention deficit hyperactivity disorder when I was younger. But now, I understand that my out-of-control behavior was just part of my response to years and years of abuse and a complete lack of boundaries in my family. With my brothers and sisters, everyone had to fend for themselves."

In treatment, clients learn to recognize the warning signs of unhealthy relationships and boundary violations and are educated about the choices available to them, with self-protection, safety, respect, and self-dignity recognized as top priorities. They learn when it is important to say no and how to say no—what words to use and how to call in support when needed. After many years of captivity, my client who had managed to escape from a human trafficking operation expressed a desire to learn how to fight and protect herself. I referred her to a local self-defense course where she learned to defend herself against all kinds of attacks. Her self-confidence grew with every class, every maneuver she learned, and every triumph she celebrated.

Without that sense of self-confidence, people sometimes attempt to keep themselves safe by trying to stay small, invisible,

When traumatized children are restless and aggressive, they often get labeled as "bad," and their suffering gets missed.

| | N |
| | N |
I work and play Well With others

| | N |
| | N |
I Keep my hands to myself

| | Y |
| | Y |
I hang up my clothes

* Michael's kindergarten report card

and submissive. They do not want to attract any attention and may dress in ways—wearing oversized clothing and dull, monochromatic colors—that allow them to fade into the woodwork. Sometimes, when that doesn't work, survivors try an opposite strategy. They identify with the bully, join a gang, or become the sexual aggressor. They become promiscuous and flirt with danger in order to look or feel strong and powerful, even though parts of them continue to feel terrified and deeply unworthy.

WHEN WE CAN'T ACKNOWLEDGE OUR FEAR —
Excessive Risk Taking and Promiscuity

Some people defend against fear and phobias by running toward danger and challenges. Rather than being afraid, they operate from a paradigm of *I'm going to face the world head-on and show everybody I'm not afraid of anything.* They live for the chase and are motivated by the notion of conquest.

I've had clients from abusive backgrounds who signed up for the military because they were looking to show that they were strong and tough. And I've seen young gay men raised in unsupportive families who put themselves in dangerous situations because they wanted to show that they could handle it, that they were "masculine enough."

I also see this frequently in my clients who work as first responders, participate in extreme sports, and actively pursue risky but exciting sexual encounters. Many find that these intense activities allow them to feel "something" when they are used to feeling nothing at all most of the time. Others seem to be overcompensating for being held in a prolonged fear state in childhood, way past their brain's upper limit for stress. In adulthood, they find roles or activities that allow them to feel powerful and effective, rather than afraid. They manage to operate from a somewhat dissociated, fierce part of themselves while totally ignoring the parts that carry the old feelings of terror and powerlessness. They learn, though, that they can keep running for only a finite period of time. Eventually, the disavowed terror and feelings of helplessness surface and need to get processed in treatment.

RESILIENCE — *The Triumph of the Human Spirit*

I want to end here with the good news: that out of adversity comes resilience. As the poet, writer, director, professor, and civil rights activist Maya Angelou wrote, "You may not control all the events that happen to you, but you can decide not to be reduced by them." Ms. Angelou didn't just survive the trauma of her early years; she managed to create a life that was absolutely magnificent. For so many, she is a symbol of true resilience.

In psychology, resilience is defined as the ability to adapt well in the face of significant stress, trauma, adversity, or loss. It's the capacity to bounce back and even flourish after difficult experiences, and often it can involve profound personal growth. It reflects flexibility and creativity in the process of overcoming difficulties. I treat artists who have used their talents as a way to work through their traumatic pasts. I see people who developed a trade or skill because they needed to do something with their hands to stay grounded and connected to the earth. I hear the stories of individuals who needed to find a way out of their communities or their families, so they committed themselves to doing well in school and managed to accomplish extraordinary things. And in 2020, during the height of the coronavirus pandemic, we heard of

To avoid feeling numb or powerless, survivors sometimes engage in high-risk behaviors.

many, many acts of kindness, moments of grace, and examples of breathtaking courage. Out of hardship and in the face of great tragedy, we discovered our resilience and ever-expanding potential for adaptation, growth, and compassion.

In Michael's case, he was pushing so much down and relying so heavily on dissociation that he couldn't read—his brain was just too stressed, too scrambled. As a result, he developed a love of all things visual; his gift for communicating through images became his professional calling card. And this love ultimately gave rise to the idea for a visually compelling book about trauma and EMDR therapy that became the book you are now holding.

The greatest blessing in my work comes from these moments of beholding what people have made of their lives, despite what or where they've come from. I get to bear witness as they find their true selves and arrive at important decisions about their present and future—*I will never, ever be like my parents. I'm going to leave all the old messages behind, and I'm going to heal myself. I am in pursuit of my own personal truth, and I'm going to share this truth with my kids. I'm going to put an end to this intergenerational cycle of trauma. It stops here.* It's just stunning to me how people make that commitment to heal their most wounded parts and to give to their families in ways that were never shown to them in their childhoods.

3

How Does Trauma Affect Your Brain?

Michael: There were clues. Cues. Buoys. I had this fragment of a memory that would come to me uninvited—sometimes several times a week—of my mother giving me a bath when I was a boy: four inches of water in the tub; the sound of the water drops hitting the water when she squeezed the washcloth, and some sensory awareness that she was washing my body—the details, images, and sounds amplified, as if they were all in high definition. I just never understood why this particular memory was so vivid and haunting.

I also had two recurring nightmares after college. In the first, I'd been an accomplice to a murder, and the police had discovered it and were coming to get me. There was no way I could hide or escape—they were going to get me and put me in prison, and I was never, ever going to get out. I would wake up soaked with sweat, shaking, and it would take me several minutes to realize it was "just" a nightmare.

In the other, I was at the top of the Empire State Building and scared to death of the height, terrified I was going to fall off. And then I did, all the way down to the ground, landing flat on the pavement, feeling the *thud* as I hit.

Trauma leaves buoys in the conscious mind—fragments of memories from unprocessed traumatic events.

But I had no idea what the memory fragments and nightmares meant, what they were connected to, or what, if any, significance they had.

Debbie: One of the most important lessons you can take from this book is that trauma and post-traumatic stress symptoms reflect injuries to our brain. If we had a sprained ankle, we wouldn't berate ourselves for not being able to run a marathon at our best time. If we couldn't digest gluten, we wouldn't be angry with ourselves for getting nauseated after eating a sandwich. Yet when people don't understand that parts of their brains are essentially sprained or intolerant, stressed beyond all reasonable limits, or repeatedly inflamed past the point of coping, they get angry with themselves. They ask themselves why they can't just be like everyone else and why they can't do the things everyone else can seemingly do. Well, it's because something in their life overwhelmed them, and their brain took a hit. It responded and then adapted in the best way it could. But despite its best attempts, it remains poorly regulated, performing at a suboptimal level. In this chapter, you'll see how our brains respond to traumatic events. And then, we'll begin to explore how to undo or reverse the dysfunctional aspects of those adaptations. Because they *can, indeed,* be reversed.

DURING A TRAUMATIC EVENT

In thinking about the brain's response to trauma, it helps to view the brain as being made up of three smaller brains: the thinking brain, the emotional brain, and the instinctual brain. The thinking brain, located at the front and top of the brain, is responsible for our being rational and logical, and for our ability to use language, imagination, and creativity, to plan and problem-solve. The emotional brain, located in the physical center of the brain, responds to nonverbal emotional and relational experiences. Lastly, the instinctual brain, located at the bottom of the brain, controls basic bodily functions such as breathing and heart rate.

The Three-Part Brain

Thinking Brain
Thinking, talking, remembering, reasoning, creating

Emotional Brain
Feeling, remembering, detecting threat, interacting with others

Instinctual Brain
Sleeping, eating, breathing, heart rate, blood pressure

When a threat is detected, the first brain region to respond is the emotional brain. The amygdala, a tiny structure within the emotional brain, functions as a threat detector and emotional command center. When the amygdala recognizes danger, it sends a distress signal to a second neighboring structure, the hypothalamus. The hypothalamus is charged with keeping our body in a balanced state and shifting states when needed. It controls our body temperature, thirst, appetite, heart rate, and blood pressure, and even our wake-sleep cycle and sex drive. When a threat signal is received from the amygdala, the hypothalamus responds by stimulating production of stress hormones and activating the

We can no more act
normally with an injured
brain than we can walk
normally on a broken leg.

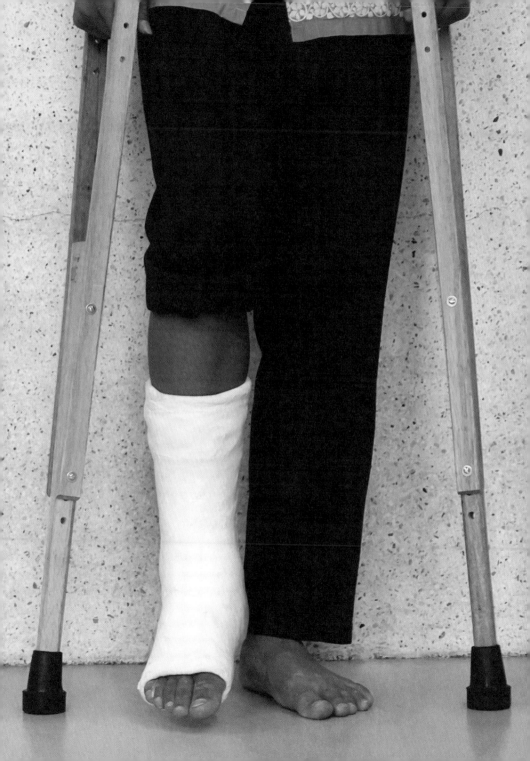

sympathetic nervous system, initiating active defensive responses via the instinctual brain. Our heart rate increases, airways open wider, blood flow to the digestive system is redirected to our muscles, our pupils dilate, and our mouth goes dry. We become speechless and begin to sweat, the hairs on our arms and neck stand on end, and, because of the increase in heart rate, additional oxygen is sped to muscle tissue to provide the energy necessary for a rapid physical response. All of this happens automatically, without any intention on our part.

The amygdala also sends signals up to the thinking brain. Then, without our awareness or permission, attention becomes more focused as our brain performs triage on incoming sensations, identifying those that most critically need our attention. The visual cortex, which processes incoming visual information, becomes hyperactive. At the same time, the thinking brain's "executive control network" is suppressed, cutting the rationally thinking "you" out of the decision-making loop. The part of the thinking brain that produces speech also slows or shuts down, which is why many trauma victims report that they were not able to scream, or yell for help, or even shout "No!" at their perpetrators. (Interestingly, a similar shutdown explains why survivors, when triggered, often have a hard time putting words to their experiences and are unable to describe the painful events that they've been through.) At times of great danger, it's important for the thinking brain to step back and allow the emotional brain to respond quickly and strongly. Only later is it safe for it to come back and retake control.

What happens next starts with a rapid orienting response. Our body freezes as we scan the environment, assess the danger, and try to identify escape routes. This is a state of high arousal but no action (again, the deer in the headlights). It is an instinctual reaction to the perception of danger, so rapid that it typically begins even before we become conscious of the threat. When escape routes *are* identified, the initial freeze shifts to either fight or flight. But for those who find themselves in threatening situations over and over again, freeze, fight, and flight can become chronic states rather than temporary ones. These chronic states can be seen in the symptoms—pervasive anxiety, flashbacks, difficulty with self-regulation, dissociation, irritability, aggression, and avoidance behaviors—of PTSD and various complex traumatic stress disorders (*e.g.*, complex PTSD and dissociative disorders). Finally, when facing particularly prolonged and inescapable interpersonal trauma, as in childhood abuse or neglect, a person's nervous system may shift instinctively into a shut down or collapse mode. This is the "feigned death" or "playing possum" reaction that we discussed in Chapter 2. Many aspects of complex traumatic stress disorders reflect this chronic state of collapse or immobilization—despair, hopelessness, paralysis, numbing, and more extreme dissociation. Over time, many trauma survivors find themselves alternating between states of freeze, fight, flight, and collapse.

Much of the dysregulation after a traumatic event is a consequence of the emotional brain continuing to hijack the thinking brain's functions. This is why we react so strongly when triggered by reminders of a traumatic event. In these situations, the thinking brain once again goes offline; we're not able to stop, orient, and evaluate whether something or someone is actually a true threat. Many consider the instinctual brain to be part of the emotional brain, because the two work so closely together. Going forward, we'll accept this idea and talk about just the thinking and emotional brains.

First and foremost,

PTSD is a brain injury.

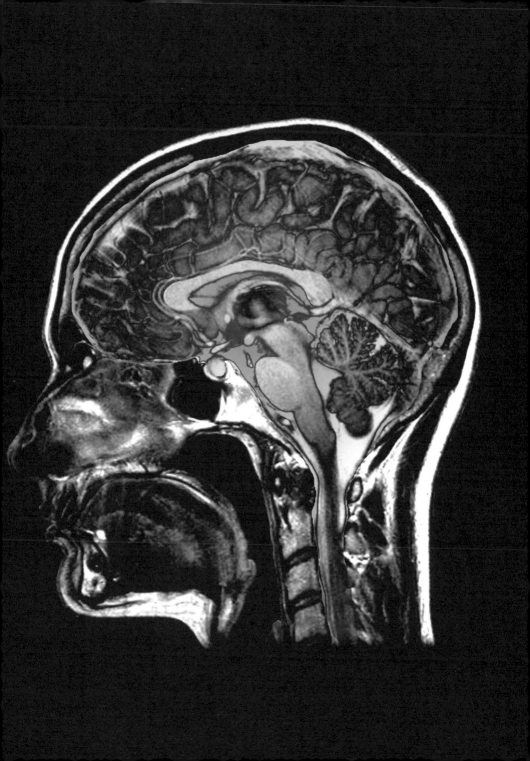

EARLY STAGES OF TRAUMA PROCESSING IN THE BRAIN

After an immediate threat has passed, the amygdala sends an "all clear" signal to the rest of the brain, telling the hypothalamus to shut off its activation of the sympathetic nervous system (fight, flight, or freeze) and to turn on the parasympathetic nervous system (*You're safe now—relax*). The parasympathetic response increases salivation, slows our heartbeat, lowers our blood pressure, constricts our pupils, and restores blood flow to our digestive system, leading us to experience relief and relaxation. At the same time, our attention becomes less focused and our arousal level drops back to normal.

Later, maybe we talk about our experience with our partner, write about it in our journal, or reflect on it as we prepare for bed, and then we "sleep on it," letting our brain review and process, and even dream about, the traumatic experience. Whatever the case, under the best of circumstances, we manage to process the experience and move on with our lives, taking what we've learned into the future to help with planning and decision-making, to help us stay safe, to get our needs met, and to make wise decisions about whom to invite or not invite into our orbit. Along the way, we probably also learn something about ourselves and the people around us, come to some realizations about our past and present circumstances, and contemplate how we might deal with similar situations in the future.

That's the ideal recovery scenario. But sometimes our brain fails to perform this post-event processing. We're still not sure why this happens. Maybe the brain is simply too stressed and dysregulated to effectively engage and process the memory. Or maybe our brain walls off the memory into an isolated, or "dissociated," neural network, so we don't even know that it's there. What we do know is that this failure has consequences.

First and foremost, the amygdala remains hyperactive, albeit at a lower level, continuing to send signals to the hypothalamus and keeping our brain and body in a state of hyper-arousal. We remain tense and hyper-alert to any signals from our environment that remind us of the traumatic event. But perhaps most catastrophic is our brain's failure to engage in the normal processing of the traumatic event. Without this processing, the memory of the event remains "frozen" in its original form, constantly reminding us and our amygdala of this perceived threat. Unable to "move beyond" the traumatic event, we remain at risk for developing PTSD or other trauma-related emotional problems. Perhaps we find ourselves engaging in outdated survival behaviors that likely don't serve us so well anymore. With prolonged or repetitive trauma, we become more and more vulnerable to developing complex PTSD or, perhaps, a dissociative disorder.

CHILDHOOD NEGLECT AND THE BRAIN

You might think that exposure to neglect and deprivation would be less detrimental to a child's brain than exposure to "acts of commission" such as physical, emotional, or sexual abuse. But neglect can become a serious issue when caregivers are overwhelmed by other demands in their lives, do not know how to be supportive, or deliberately and regularly shun or abandon a child as a form of punishment. They might be physically or emotionally unavailable because of work demands, military service, incarceration, addiction, physical or mental illness, dissociation, or extreme family stress. Neglect can also result when a child is frequently moved from one unstable environment to another (such as foster care) or is living in an institutional setting with many other

Trauma can also be caused
by neglect, deprivation,
or a lack of nurturing.

children, few caregivers, and no actual one-on-one responsive adult interactions.

Though this kind of trauma may be quieter and perhaps less shocking, its effects on a child's brain are usually similar to those produced by more blatant acts of commission. Childhood neglect engenders the same fears, perceptions of danger, and feelings of helplessness and despair as those seen with more dramatic forms of abuse.

As a result, we can expect the same responses from the brain— the same initial stress response, the same failure of the stress response to subside with time, and the same failure of normal memory processing. When fear, being overwhelmed, and a sense of aloneness are particularly intense or chronic, we might also expect to see extreme dissociative responses and signs of psychological shutdown. Remember, a child in her home often has no possibility of physical escape, so psychological escape becomes the only option.

Acts of neglect (and of other, more active forms of abuse) often occur over and over, across extended periods of a child's early life. This is a developmental period when the brain is still growing and maturing and laying down the basic neural connections for behavior and coping under a variety of circumstances. Excessive activation of stress response systems during this time can have damaging effects on developing brain circuitry. Research tells us that young children affected by neglect and deprivation suffer more pervasive developmental impairments than those exposed to overt physical abuse, including increased risks for attentional, emotional, cognitive, interpersonal, and behavioral problems, as well as learning difficulties and underachievement in school. Without comprehensive and effective intervention along the way, these children may enter their teens and then adulthood with the kinds of trauma-related symptoms described within these pages.

Once again, what starts as a brain injury and a breakdown of the brain's information processing system ends up as pervasive dysregulation across many, many areas of a person's life. To better understand why this breakdown in information processing occurs, we need to back up and look at how memory processing happens in the first place, starting with the very nature of memory.

THE NATURE OF MEMORY

We usually think of a memory as something like a photograph or movie—clear, concise, and self-contained—a single object stored somewhere in our brain. But it's not that simple. For a start, there are different memory storage systems in the brain. To understand why PTSD develops, we need to understand the differences between them. The explicit memory system stores memories we can consciously recall—often with the ability to see them in our mind's eye as if they were, indeed, photos or movies. In contrast, the implicit system stores memories that we can't consciously recall.

Explicit memories are ones that can be brought back into our conscious awareness, ones that we can report. They include memories of what we had for breakfast, a conversation last night with a friend, where we left our car keys (we hope, anyway!), and what's on our schedule for today. They're the memories of our first date, our first kiss, and the birth of our first child, as well as the memories of a play or sports event we attended. And they're the memories from our traumatic past, or at least those portions of the memories that we can remember or replay in our mind.

But there are parts of these memories, especially from traumatic events, that we can't easily bring to mind, that we don't even know are there. A good example of the distinction between explicit

Traumatic events can overload our emotional "circuit breakers."

and implicit memories is learning to ride a bike. You might have an explicit, autobiographical memory of your mom or dad holding your bike while you learned to keep your balance. But that is separate from the actual "procedural" memory you have of how to ride it. We sometimes call memories like this one muscle memories, as if they were stored in your muscles and not your brain. But of course, they actually are stored in your brain. You just can't *see* them—they don't come with a picture. We call memories like this implicit memories, because the only way we know they're there is because our behavior *implies* that they must be. If you made it around that curve on your bike, you must have a memory of how to do it.

Why are we spending so much time describing this? Because memories of traumatic events are often implicit. They're implied by a strong physical reaction to a normally innocuous smell or sound or sight, or by compulsive or repetitive patterns of responding to authority figures. Very often, clients have no idea why they're reacting in a particular way or making a decision that has no explicit memory to justify it. As my client Dee asked at the start of treatment, "Why would I be deathly afraid of crowds, swimming underwater, or having an MRI? It's so random. I can't find anything in my history that explains why I get so afraid in these situations." As a trauma therapist, I've learned that strong reactions and uncharacteristic behaviors (*I can't believe I reacted that way. That's really not like me at all!*) offer clues to memories of important experiences my clients may not remember or, if remembered, may not recognize as relevant. For Dee, early EMDR-focused explorations led us to some childhood memories: getting separated from her parents at a crowded state fair, being knocked over and tumbled by a huge wave at the beach, and feeling trapped, terrified, and alone in a small room when she had her tonsils removed. Bringing these memories into explicit consciousness, and then processing them, alleviated her phobias and dramatically increased her sense of security and choice in her day-to-day life.

Michael's memories were also mostly implicit, affecting him from some hidden corner of his mind. Like Dee's, their existence was clearly implied by his behaviors: running away from women who were interested in him, avoiding public bathrooms, doting on his mother at his own expense, tangling with authority figures, being a perfectionist in an attempt to gain praise and ward off criticism and rejection from others.

When I teach, I use the model of a massive island in the middle of the ocean where only a few acres are above the waterline. When therapists work with just that tip, never looking deeper, their clients never come to understand the vast terrain of implicit memory. Therapists need to be radically curious and look for clues in the body, speech, and behaviors of their clients so they can get to the rest of the story, to the hidden parts of their clients' experiences and memories—because without the whole story, we can solve only part of the problem. This is what Michael encountered in his life. Despite many attempts at psychotherapy, dissociated experiences held by his body and expressed through his behavior were never brought into conscious awareness. That changed once he met Dr. Magnavita and started EMDR therapy. For the first time, with ample support and safety, he could tolerate recalling these experiences, and the implicit was finally made explicit.

HOW MEMORY PROCESSING NORMALLY WORKS

On some level, we all know that memories change over time. Think of those arguments you've had with partners, coworkers, or friends about some event in the past. Often, you'll disagree on where something happened, who else was there, what exactly happened, or what was said. It almost feels like you're talking about two different events. And it's not just that pieces are *missing* from one of your memories. It seems like the memories themselves have *actually changed*. That's because they have. You truly do remember it differently from how you did at an earlier time, which is not necessarily a bad thing. Memories *evolve* over time through a series of brain processes aimed at producing a version of the memory that will be most useful to you in the future. Although your brain keeps the emotional core, it might forget some of the details, and you might find that your body responds with less distress to this newer version of the memory. Your brain also finds connections to related memories or information, which provide a context for reinterpreting the meaning and significance of events.

Ideally, in the case of trauma memories, this processing leads to greater clarity about the traumatic events. We reorient from the past to the present and future, and it becomes safe for us to leave the events and their memories behind. It's an impressively effective process, and the vast majority of our traumatic memories are successfully dealt with in this manner. But for some people and some events, this brain mechanism fails. And it's the outsized consequences of these failures that we are focusing on in this book.

WHEN MEMORY PROCESSING GETS STUCK

When someone experiences an overwhelming traumatic event or one that somehow leaves them feeling powerless and vulnerable, all of these elegant brain processes can stall out, leaving the memory frozen in its original, raw form. The details surrounding the core emotional aspects are retained in vivid Technicolor; they are not dimmed by time. And our response to recalling the event remains as powerful as when it first occurred. At the same time, the memory of that event fails to link up with other, related memories—those from before and after—that might help us understand what the event means and how we need to shift our perspective and our reactions to help us heal. And so, the memory remains a moment of terror frozen in time, as isolated from the rest of our memories as, perhaps, we feel isolated from the rest of the world post-trauma—caught between past and present, often confused, and feeling deeply alienated from everyone around us. To understand why this happens, you need to first understand a brain process known as neuroplasticity.

"NEURONS THAT FIRE TOGETHER WIRE TOGETHER"

The brain is an ever-evolving entity that changes from one second to the next; it has an incredible quality called neuroplasticity. Most simply put, neuroplasticity is the ability of nerve cells, or neurons, in the brain to change how they behave. It is the brain's ability to restructure itself by establishing new neural pathways as needed. The nature of this plasticity was first described by the neuropsychologist Donald Hebb, back in 1949. He is best known for saying, "Neurons that fire together wire together." As an example of how this works, consider the expression "Roses are red, violets are blue." We've all heard it so many times that if someone says, "Roses are red," we all think, *Violets are blue.* Hearing this over and over actually wired together these phrases in our brain. We have thousands of these associations that have become wired in our brain, which is mostly a good thing. But this concept also

Trauma can create
an unconscious
"magnetic field"—
a powerful attraction
to familiar personalities
and patterns.

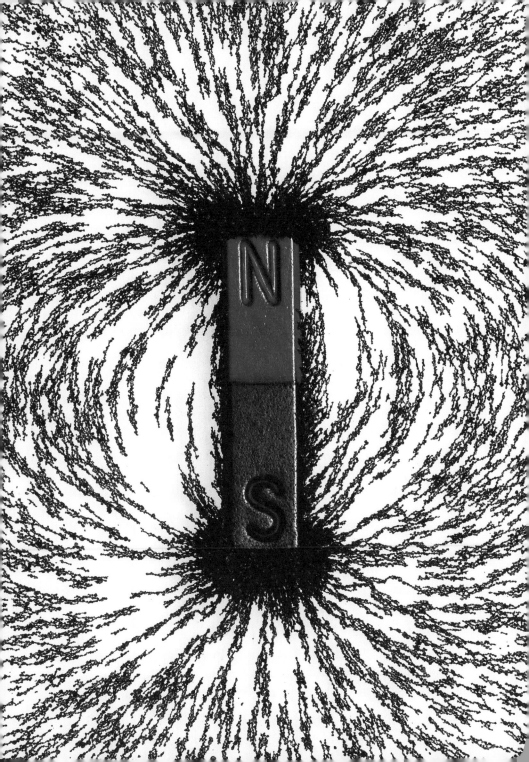

explains how triggers become wired to trauma memories. As a result, every time we encounter a trigger, it activates the spontaneous replay of a memory, and that in turn further strengthens the neural connection between trigger and memory. Trauma survivors grow anxious when confronted with reminders of past traumas and, over time, that fear generalizes to more and more situations. These new situations eventually create their own unique neural pathways, connecting present day people, places, and things with trauma-based fear reactions.

Yes, neurons that fire together wire together. You may have seen the consequences in your own behavior. Somehow, every time you get into certain situations, you act as you have a thousand times before, even though you've promised yourself that you'll handle things differently the next time. Very often, trauma survivors find themselves repeating patterns that they know, on one level, are not healthy or are even potentially dangerous: returning to an abusive relationship, picking up an alcoholic drink, shutting down or remaining silent, freezing like a deer in the headlights, beating themselves up for not being perfect. The list can seem endless. We all understand that knowing something or committing to something in our thinking brain does not necessarily mean that we can easily use that knowledge to help us control our behavior or emotional reactions. Learned patterns of behavior that become hardwired in our emotional brain are so powerful, they can compel us to respond in ways that we know are not in our own best interest.

However, we now know that every time you reactivate one of these learned behavior patterns—one of these constantly reinforced brain associations—the brain connections that underlie them become malleable and open to change. In EMDR therapy, we intentionally reactivate the memories linked to problematic beliefs, behaviors, and symptoms so we can change them, diminishing or even eliminating reactions to triggers. When we reactivate these memories, contradictory information—evidence that we are, indeed, "good enough," safe, and no longer powerless—often spontaneously comes to mind. Actively noticing this new information while simultaneously holding the trauma memory in mind actually weakens the connection between trigger and reaction, reducing the associated distress and changing the meaning of that memory. And it's through these changes that memory evolution occurs, allowing you to heal—reducing symptoms, changing unhealthy patterns of behavior, and slowly moving you from the past fully into the present.

So, bottom line: Even though the traumatized brain has limited mental flexibility and imagination and can sometimes leave you stuck in the rut of overlearned, *overwired* behavior patterns, neuroplasticity offers us hope for change and a new path forward.

THE NEUROBIOLOGY OF RECOVERY

In the clinical and scientific communities, our efforts to better understand trauma and the brain have led us to think in novel ways about what's required for comprehensive healing. When we reflect on the role of dissociation and the many forms of dysregulation (emotional, behavioral, somatic, relational, attentional) associated with trauma, and we recognize how trauma-related disorders represent a breakdown of the normal memory processing system of the brain, it becomes increasingly clear that several things need to happen in therapy to achieve a full recovery. In EMDR therapy, we pay particular attention to each of these needs.

When repeatedly exposed
to inescapable trauma,
our bodies can get stuck in
a chronic state of freeze.

First, we need to get the brain into an optimal arousal state. Let's do a quick review from chapter 2 with brain physiology in mind. My traumatized clients tend to fluctuate between states of hyper-arousal and hypo-arousal. In hyper-arousal, their sympathetic nervous system—the accelerator—is fully engaged, and their emotional brain is firing on all cylinders. They're on guard and scanning for danger with active defenses primed. Sometimes they exhibit pressured speech, signs of extreme anxiety and panic, and disorganized, fragmented thinking. Many are in a chronic freeze state.

In contrast, when their brain shifts into hypo-arousal, their parasympathetic nervous system—the body's brake—becomes fully engaged and we see a major shutdown of emotional experience accompanied by dissociation, numbing, and behavioral slowing or immobilization. Clients sometimes appear collapsed and report that they feel completely disconnected from their bodies. At still other times, it may seem as if they're hitting the gas and the brakes at the same time. They're agitated, but frozen and unable to speak or move their bodies without great effort.

Learning and transformation cannot happen until clients are able to return to an optimal arousal state. This means getting parts of the thinking brain rebooted and back online and getting the thinking and emotional brains working together in an integrated way. Sometimes I'll introduce coping skills (for example, diaphragmatic breathing, mindfulness, guided imagery, strategies for staying oriented to current time and place) to help my clients find and remain in this optimal zone, widening their personal window of tolerance so they can stay present and grounded in the face of increased arousal, instead of becoming overwhelmed, shutting down, or dissociating. Finding that balance between the emotional and the thinking brain is key. With greater self-regulation, clients are able to simply observe memories as they arise, rather than being hijacked by overwhelming emotions or physical distress.

Once the client has achieved a sufficiently wide window of tolerance, traumatic memories—isolated and frozen in time with all their associated information—need to be accessed and processed. In EMDR therapy, we activate traumatic memories while simultaneously accessing other relevant information and memories, allowing new perspectives, experiences, and messages to be purposefully integrated with the trauma memory.

By accessing a trauma memory while remaining in the therapeutic window of tolerance, you can know and feel and reflect on your own story. You can bear witness to your pain, and by doing so, the pain is transformed. The resolved memory slides into the past, shifting, for the first time, into its proper place in your personal story. Rather than seeing the abuse and neglect in her childhood as her fault, my college-age client now understands that her parents were both very ill and incapable of caring for her. She no longer feels shame and guilt, but instead, pride in her resilience and post-traumatic accomplishments. When my veteran reflects on his inability to save his buddy from a deadly ambush, he no longer collapses into despair, overcome with a desire to die. Now he recognizes that there was, indeed, nothing he could have done to save his friend and that he, in fact, acted courageously that day to protect his fellow soldiers. With EMDR processing, trauma memories are adaptively resolved and returned to storage in an altered, more useful form, allowing symptoms to fade away.

Traditional talk therapy
is limited in its ability
to treat trauma.

LIMITATIONS OF TRADITIONAL TALK THERAPY

Simply telling the story of what happened, describing symptoms or feelings, or reflecting on what it all means, isn't usually enough to achieve real change. Yes, having a safe, supportive environment where you receive understanding, validation, and perspective, and where someone bears witness to your story, definitely matters and is something that every therapist I know strives to provide. But that alone is often not enough to quell the involuntary, biologically driven, physiological and hormonal responses of the body and the brain. Although the intellectual mind may know that it is safe to talk and feel and remember, the deeper structures of the brain may not. And verbal exploration and sharing alone are not enough to transform the traumatic memories that are continuing to cause distress and debilitating symptoms.

At the start of treatment, clients may find themselves sharing their "cover stories"—accounts about themselves, their families, and their lives that they have told many times before, rather than focusing on what they are experiencing emotionally and physically in the moment. Many are simply too scared to attend to their emotional experiences, let alone their most traumatic memories, in session. And though they yearn for comfort and support, their brain does not allow them to calm down and connect, internally or externally. So they remain on guard—terrified of being hurt, overwhelmed, or abandoned.

Others are simply too flooded with emotion and distress to even *try* to describe or discuss relevant experiences, past or present. As they attempt to address uncomfortable issues, they get hit out of left field with a groundswell of emotional pain and find themselves unable to maintain any kind of observing stance. Sometimes they even feel worse at the end of a session rather than better. These are the kinds of descriptions that I have heard over the years about people's previous therapy experiences. Perhaps you recognize yourself in one of these descriptions. And perhaps you have also felt that you've come up short in previous psychotherapies or that you're "just not good at it."

Judith, an extremely bright and articulate college professor, sought treatment with me after decades in traditional talk therapy with one therapist after another. At our initial session, she reported that she was still haunted by intrusive incest memories and that social anxiety, shame, and self-hatred kept her from developing friendships and pursuing her creative and academic interests. I will never forget her words: "All the insight in the world has not quieted the alarms going off in my nervous system. My brain still feels like it's on fire. I don't ever really feel safe in the presence of others. I have shared my story dozens of times, but it's always as if I'm talking about someone else. And things don't change—not really. I know that I need to approach things differently this time."

Effective trauma-informed therapies, like EMDR, include both "top-down" and "bottom-up" approaches to healing. Traditional talk therapy is considered a top-down approach because it requires accessing higher-level areas of the thinking brain responsible for verbal memory. In top-down therapies, words are used to regulate non-verbal emotional and body-based experiences. The starting point is the client's story, and the focus is on evoking the emotions connected to past events, meaning-making, and getting to a better understanding of oneself and one's life. As insight increases, the hope is that one's self-narrative and relationship to past experiences will also change.

But this top-down approach, emphasizing verbal exploration, reflection, and cognitive strategies, can only be effective when a client's thinking brain is fully online and operative. Because trauma-related responses inhibit the thinking brain, keeping it online and operative is often impossible for clients, especially at the start of treatment. And later in treatment, it can be difficult to fully access and transform implicit fears, messages, and memories without prioritizing nonverbal emotional and body experience.

A "bottom-up" approach does not rule out narrative retelling or insight, but works primarily with the body's visceral responses to the activation of traumatic memories in the emotional brain. What is different is that we start with sensations and movements; understanding and meaning are derived from new body-based and emotional experiences, not vice versa. A greater sense of confidence in regulating trauma responses also emerges from experiencing bodily and emotional shifts. (*I now* feel *bigger, stronger, safer, and more in control.*) When working from the bottom up with a client, I strive to create experiences that contradict the sense of helplessness and vulnerability, the impulse to flee when there is, in fact, no danger, or to collapse when it's important to remain alert and active. At all times, I carefully modulate the sound of my voice, the pace of my speech, my eye contact, where I sit relative to my client, and the rhythm of my words—so that the emotional brain will register safety and security and know that it's okay to relax and actually be still while remaining alert. This moment-to-moment coordination and co-regulation—involving both verbal and nonverbal communication and a collaborative effort to stay within the window of tolerance—is essential as we work together to prepare for trauma-focused work.

Once we've achieved this, we're ready for the next step—confronting and processing relevant traumatic experiences. Our mission: to deactivate and transform the trauma memories that are causing ongoing symptoms. If we succeed in changing the way my client relates to her memories, we change the way she experiences the world, herself, and others.

EMDR therapy offers an elegant treatment model, using an integrated top-down/bottom-up approach. A session may begin with a focus on your story, but then it shifts to studying your internal experience. You get lots of practice in cognitively, emotionally, and somatically tracking changes in your internal experience while simultaneously being encouraged to find the words to describe them. You are invited to experiment with new actions, new perspectives, and new words. The therapist helps you regulate your emotions through a compassionate, nonverbal presence, information sharing, skill development, and supportive words and actions. As you have new experiences, you reflect on them with your therapist, arriving at new insights and venturing back out into the world to pursue new opportunities. In many different ways, EMDR restores the healthy, balanced interplay among the three parts of your brain—thinking, emotional, and instinctual—and addresses what you need to transform your inner experience, relationships, and day-to-day life.

EMDR therapy pinpoints
traumatic memories,
so they can finally be
fully processed.

4

What Is EMDR Therapy, and How Does It Work?

Michael: In my sixties, after a lifetime of therapy that did little to resolve my problems, without a job that allowed me to take some cover from my demons, and without healthy relationships that could support and challenge me, I was at an emotional crossroads, afraid I was headed toward the darkest path. Then, my sisters intervened.

My younger sister said, "You are way too involved with Mom. It isn't healthy—or normal."

And my older sister said, "There is a therapist, Dr. Magnavita, who is amazing. Are you serious about wanting to get help or not?"

So, on March 24, 2017, I drove two and a half hours to Glastonbury, Connecticut, to meet the man who would introduce me to EMDR therapy and save my life.

Debbie: So, how exactly does EMDR therapy *work*? During EMDR therapy, a client is directed to focus internally on a traumatic memory or trigger while engaged in bilateral stimulation (sometimes referred to as BLS). *Bilateral* in this case means simply "back and forth"—typically, moving the eyes side to side while tracking an external stimulus, like the therapist's fingers or a moving light. This creates a condition of "dual attention"—a simultaneous focus on an external activity *and* an internal memory or experience—that seems to jump-start and support the processing of the memory. Although eye movements are the type of bilateral stimulation most widely used and the form most supported by research, other forms of bilateral stimulation can be employed, such as tones delivered through headphones or handheld pulsars or even knee taps. However, if it were just about bilateral stimulation, every trauma survivor at a tennis match would be spontaneously healed. Or they could simply sit in their cars and watch their windshield wipers go back and forth.

There are, in fact, many other elements to EMDR therapy. The therapist assists the client in choosing the best "target" to focus on and helps him fully "activate" that target—i.e., memory of a traumatic experience or trigger situation—before introducing bilateral stimulation. The therapist also actively helps the client remain attentive to whatever emerges: images, thoughts, emotions, physical sensations and impulses, and previously dissociated fragments of memory. It is the therapist's presence and careful attention to keeping her client within his window of tolerance—while confronting memories—that is key. Dr. Shapiro initially thought that she had simply created an approach to reducing anxiety, but she later came to realize that EMDR offered much more. In a nutshell, when clients reprocess traumatic memories and triggers, they are able to reduce distress *and* come to terms with significant guilt, shame, unmet needs, grief, and anger while addressing their sense of defectiveness, vulnerability, and powerlessness.

A substantial number of randomized controlled trials support the positive effects of the eye movement component of EMDR.

Bilateral stimulation—back-and-forth movements—jump-starts the processing of memories.

But what do the eye movements actually do? Researchers have found that they alter how our brains normally process memories and emotions. Eye movements seem to reduce the intensity of the negative emotions, as well as the vividness of the associated visual imagery. They seem to improve our ability to recall memories. They lower our emotional arousal and help us relax. And they help us break out of patterns of rigid, focused thinking. All of these effects are potentially helpful when we're trying to resolve distress related to traumatic memories.

How the eye movements produce these effects, and how they help with processing traumatic memories, is less clear. Researchers have come up with a lot of theories on the subject, but most of the attention of researchers and clinicians has been focused on three of these theories. From the very beginning, Francine Shapiro favored the REM Sleep model, which suggests that moving the eyes triggers a state similar to REM sleep, when our eyes jump back and forth to the left and right. During REM sleep, our brain (1) reduces the negative emotions associated with memories, (2) thinks more flexibly, building new associations between our memories, and (3) is better at gaining insight and understanding from these new associations, just like during an EMDR session.

A second model is referred to as the Orienting Response model. According to this model's hypothesis, the act of orienting to a moving target forces the brain to constantly shift its attention—from one side to the other and then back again. Doing so helps the emotional brain quiet the sympathetic nervous system (responsive to threat), activating the parasympathetic system (calm and engaged) instead, and allowing the thinking brain to regain its normal role in processing incoming information. Interestingly, this shift occurs in REM sleep as well.

The third model, which has received the most attention from researchers, with more than forty studies supporting its claims, is the Working Memory model. Working memory is the system we rely on to remember an address *while* listening to directions. It's the one we use when we are holding a recipe in our mind *while* making a meal. In EMDR therapy, we are using working memory when we access and then focus on a traumatic event. But here's the key: Working memory has a limited capacity. (*Wait—did she say right at the lamppost or left?*) By asking you to track moving fingers or a moving light while focusing on a traumatic event in your mind, we are overtaxing your working memory. As a result, the traumatic memory becomes less vivid and less emotional. Preventing the brain from visualizing the recalled trauma memory as intensely and as clearly as it normally would calms the emotional brain and reduces the experience of distress.

As you might have noticed, these aren't necessarily mutually exclusive models, and it may well be that all three accurately describe aspects of the brain's response to eye movements or other forms of bilateral stimulation. What we do know is that between them, they can explain all the benefits of eye movements that we mentioned at the start of this section.

Some therapists, like Dr. Magnavita, will hold up two fingers and move them back and forth, asking the client to follow with their eyes. Some tap back and forth on their client's hands or knees. Others might use a piece of equipment called a light bar that has a small light that moves back and forth from one end to the other as a client tracks it with their eyes. Alternatively, there are various types of pulsars that clients can hold in their palms that produce vibrations that alternate back and forth between the two hands. Finally, some therapists use headphones with tones that shift from one ear to the other. No matter what form of bilateral stimulation is used, even if it doesn't involve eye movements, the treatment is still referred to as EMDR therapy. During the height of the coronavirus pandemic, when almost all psychotherapists were working virtually, we discovered that EMDR therapy can be effectively provided online with only minor adaptations to the ways in which we administer the bilateral stimulation.

Sometimes, multiple modalities are used simultaneously if that is deemed more effective for a given client. Research findings demonstrate that eye movements are more effective than tones, but other modalities have not yet been systematically examined in research settings.

So what do we mean when we refer to "processing" in an EMDR therapy session? The client—fully alert and working collaboratively with her therapist—is asked to track some form of bilateral stimulation while focusing on a traumatic memory or present-day trigger. (When clients experience recurring negative thoughts or feelings but can't easily identify associated traumatic memories, we begin with the "floatback technique," described later in this chapter, to help find relevant "target" memories.) The client begins to "process" the traumatic memories that have been active just below the surface, sometimes for years or, as in Michael's case, for decades. Typically, emotional, physical, and cognitive associations emerge spontaneously.

Processing can be thought of as accelerated learning or healing. Old experiences are reengaged, and in the course of a session, memories—with their painful images, thoughts, or beliefs, emotions, and sensations—become less disturbing; distorted perceptions or viewpoints shift, and new information and present-day adult perspectives get considered and integrated. The memory is then re-stored with the new information—*It wasn't my fault; It's over; I did the best I could; I am capable of loving again in the future*—together with new, more positive emotions and experiences, such as self-compassion, pride, triumph, or relief. The memory is then available in its altered form as a source of information for future action and decision-making. The person's body and physiology find a new equilibrium and sense of safety in the present while a faulty, hyper-reactive alarm system cools down and the frontal lobes of the thinking brain fully come back online.

EMDR: AN OVERVIEW

In this section, as we begin to explain the phases of EMDR treatment, it is important to start by saying that trauma treatment, like any kind of healing, is not linear. We describe it with steps and stages and phases, but it's much more of an iterative, layered process. It's more of a labyrinth than a straight line. That means that clients may revisit a memory or a trigger more than once, but each time they return, it is with a deeper and more nuanced understanding of relevant issues and symptoms, more ability to integrate an adaptive adult perspective, and more resilience and self-acceptance. There is flexibility to move around and address symptoms and struggles as they arise in real time, reevaluating relevant targets as the work progresses.

That being said, there is a consensus within the field of trauma treatment that emphasizes the importance of "sequencing" clients' treatment. It is helpful to think about treatment in terms of early, middle, and later stages, with each stage having its own goals. In early sessions, we focus on establishing adequate safety, stability, and coping skills, and a good working relationship between the client

EMDR therapy is
a nonlinear process—
you know where you want
to go, but you don't know
exactly how you'll get there.

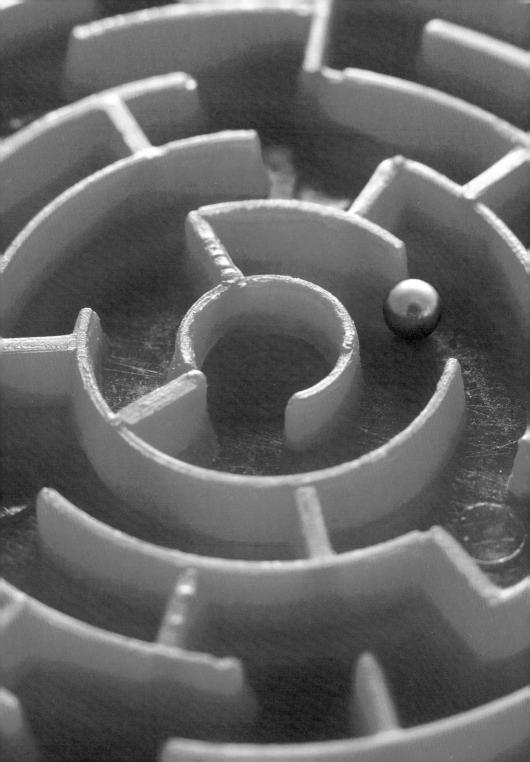

and therapist. Before focusing on traumatic memories and triggers, we want to be sure that the client can do so without shutting down or numbing out, dissociating, or becoming overwhelmed. People need to be stable enough in their lives and in the therapy office, secure enough with their therapist, and able to tolerate exposure to traumatic material and big feelings well enough before moving on to any more in-depth work. "Stable enough" means that clients can work with difficult material while remaining mostly within their window of tolerance, one foot in the present at all times while dipping into the past. They are able to safely access memories and process relevant thoughts, feelings, and bodily sensations. They're able to bring their attention to their internal experience while staying completely grounded in the here and now and connected to their therapist.

This early stage can be relatively short—perhaps one to three sessions—for a client who is seeking help after experiencing a single traumatic incident. This also might be the case for someone who has a good repertoire of coping skills and is able to comfortably attach to a therapist and tolerate strong emotion, or someone who had a relatively high level of functioning before a recent trauma or onset of symptoms. However, for those with a complex trauma history who lack adequate coping skills, those who are more prone to dissociation or have a dissociative disorder, or those who are struggling with more high-risk behaviors (such as addictions, eating disorders, suicidality or self-injury, or violence toward others), this stage will likely be more extended.

In the middle stage of treatment, once there is "enough" stabilization, the focus shifts to the client's actual traumatic experiences. Processing work directly addresses those memories frozen in the nervous system and their associated symptoms and triggers. We locate them, activate the feelings, sensations, thoughts, images, and sensory components associated with them, and work with them until they are no longer "charged" or distressing.

Finally, in the later stage of treatment, the focus is on reconnection, finding meaning, and thinking about who you are now, in the present moment, post-trauma. In the third stage of treatment, clients reflect on what they want to be doing in the present and how they want to move into the future. They're setting goals for themselves, considering initiatives, and practicing new behaviors that they've possibly never even considered before.

Dr. Magnavita could see, from the earliest moments with Michael, that he would be able to tolerate challenging trauma-focused work with his support. Despite his history of increased dissociation in response to stress and trauma-related triggers, Michael was able to stay connected to his story, to the present moment, and to Dr. Magnavita as they discussed his symptoms and adverse life experiences. With help, he was able to explore and express a range of emotions while staying within his window of tolerance. And he showed a remarkable willingness to trust Dr. Magnavita. Although he was deeply distraught and scared of what the road ahead might be like, he was motivated to work hard in therapy and displayed a readiness for change. It was evident to Dr. Magnavita, after taking a thorough history, that Michael's symptoms were rooted in early traumatic experiences, so he felt strongly about beginning EMDR processing as quickly as possible to help alleviate Michael's suffering.

Even after processing has become the focus of sessions, if a client becomes more symptomatic or is having difficulty tolerating the work for whatever reason, we may decide to slow the pace, work with smaller bites, or circle back to coping-focused work until he stabilizes and feels ready to proceed. The goal, however, is

During processing,
we work to remove the
emotional charge of
traumatic memories.

always to return to the processing work, as it is the most efficient route to reducing symptoms and distress.

That said, much depends on whether clients are living in a stable environment that supports their recovery. If they are struggling with basic safety, if they can't put food on their table, if their family or marriage is in crisis, if they're living in a country or neighborhood that's under siege, they may not have enough mental energy available for processing. If that's the case, we would first turn our attention to helping with resources, internal and/or external. External resources might include helping someone access community support or obtain financial or housing assistance. It might include a referral to a twelve-step program or some type of psychotherapy group. A focus on internal resources might involve accessing parts of themselves that possess a sense of courage, clarity, or groundedness. It might involve teaching them mindfulness skills, how to use guided imagery, or how to self-soothe.

The quality and stability of their day-to-day life can improve tremendously with this kind of effort. Then, when they're ready, we resume. Sometimes, even when someone's environment is intensely unstable, we find ways to slowly but steadily proceed with the work, because processing is what's needed to change patterns—to stop abusing substances or self-injuring, to find a way to leave a domestic violence or abusive work situation, or to leave home when home isn't a good place to be.

THE EIGHT PHASES OF EMDR THERAPY

There are eight phases to EMDR therapy:

1. History Taking and Treatment Planning

2. Preparation

3. Assessment

4. Desensitization

5. Installation

6. Body Scan

7. Closure

8. Reevaluation

Phases one and two are primarily handled during the earliest stage of treatment. Once the focus turns to trauma processing, the client repeatedly cycles through phases three through eight with each new target memory. Don't worry, though. You don't have to figure all this out. It's the EMDR therapist's responsibility to ask questions to get the lay of the land, to evaluate what to focus on in each session, and to be the tour guide. The therapist drives the bus, but the client is the co-navigator and clearly gets to weigh in on the route, the speed of travel, and when it's time for a pit stop.

PHASE 1 — *History Taking and Treatment Planning:*
Understanding the Big Picture and Coming Up with a Game Plan

When someone comes into treatment, they rarely arrive saying, "Hi, I'm here to work on my sexual abuse history from ages five through twelve." Instead, they come in saying, "I can't sleep. I'm having trouble in my relationships. I'm depressed. I can't get out of bed in the morning." So in the earliest sessions, during the history taking and treatment planning phase, there's an exploration of current symptoms and one's history and significant life events—positive, negative, and in between—going all the way back to early development. Every therapist is going to handle this exploration a little differently, but the goal in this early phase is to begin to develop an understanding of how life experiences have contributed to symptoms, behavior patterns, and difficulties in a range of areas. We're also listening for client strengths and resources (i.e., courage, determination, talents, supportive people, and role models) that can be brought into the work in some way.

I ask my clients to complete certain questionnaires about their exposure to trauma, core beliefs, symptoms of depression, anxiety, PTSD, complex PTSD, or dissociative experiences. Again, every therapist works differently, but ultimately, we're all looking for the connection between present symptoms, behavior patterns, and relational styles, and earlier adverse life experiences.

Your EMDR therapist is going to be curious about recent times when you experienced some degree of distress—perhaps the time when you last experienced the symptoms that brought you into treatment. He might ask, "When did you first start experiencing these symptoms? How far back do they go? What's the first or worst time you remember experiencing anything like that?" He may ask you to close your eyes and scan back from that recent experience. "So as you think about getting triggered by your boss this past week, feeling ashamed and wanting to run, saying to yourself, 'I'm such a loser' or 'I'm a pathetic mess—I can't do anything right,' notice what that feels like emotionally, notice where you feel it in your body, and begin to float back from that experience to the earliest time that you remember experiencing anything like that."

I typically take a piece of paper, make three columns, and write, "Past," "Present," and "Future." As I listen to the client, I jot down all the relevant past events connected to a given symptom or pattern, all the relevant present triggers, and all the proposed goals for the future. Comprehensive EMDR therapy focuses on all of these components; we desensitize past experiences and triggers and orient to tackling present and future challenges with a new, more positive sense of self.

It is not a problem if you are initially unable to identify any old memories related to your distress. When it comes time to begin processing, your EMDR therapist will simply ask you to focus on your current symptoms or triggers. Also, as your therapist is gathering history and working collaboratively with you to establish goals for treatment, he is listening and observing and evaluating your tolerance for emotionally focused work. If you start to get dysregulated—if your thinking gets disorganized, if you start to dissociate, freeze, or appear overwhelmed—he will help you engage in some kind of action to restore your equilibrium.

Whenever possible, though, your therapist will return to the symptoms, triggers, and memories that are most charged or most disabling, because, again, that's where you're going to get the biggest bang for your buck.

PHASE 2 — *Preparation: Getting Ready for Processing*

As you start treatment, there will undoubtedly be significant fears and concerns lurking right beneath the surface. Most therapists will do their best to set your mind at ease and allay your fears. I often say to people, "I want you to pay close attention to what I'm doing, how I'm engaging with you, and how it feels to be in therapy with me. And if any part of you has questions or doubts about me or about the work, I want to hear about it. I'll keep doing my best to reassure you that I'm committed to you, to this process, and to your safety and healing. We'll just keep talking about how it feels to be

To find the source of current symptoms, we float back in search of earlier, related memories.

working together." Again, every therapist has his or her own way of conveying this message.

During the preparation phase, we help our clients create an image of a safe or calm place, a place where nothing bad has ever happened. "Is there a place that you can think of, either somewhere you've been before or someplace in your imagination, that feels soothing or calming?" Then we "install" the safe place imagery. The client is asked to focus on their safe place while tracking some form of slow bilateral stimulation: several sets of ten to twelve back-and-forth movements. We check in after each one—"What do you notice now?" Interestingly, when we start with positive material or experiences and use slow bilateral stimulation, that which is positive actually tends to become more positive. Safe place imagery becomes more soothing and relaxing. Remember, the brain is wired to move toward healing and optimal health.

For people who need more resources beyond a safe place, we might do more extensive "resourcing" work. My colleague Andrew Leeds and I introduced a protocol called resource development and installation (RDI) in 2002. Over time, RDI has become a standard part of EMDR treatment, generally used when a client needs to increase their self-regulation skills. The goal of RDI is to help you identify memories associated with positive states of being. Through a series of questions, we explore times when you have felt mastery, triumph, or a particular quality such as courage or strength. We look for relationships with attachment figures who have helped you feel strong or capable or loved. If you have no relationships to directly draw from in your life (yes, this happens!), we might talk about inspiring or wise characters in books, on TV, or in movies. We might think about symbolic resources, too. As an example, I often talk about the tree outside my office that's firmly rooted in the ground, branches reaching for the sky, flexible in the wind but solid. These resources are "installed" with bilateral stimulation, just like we do with safe place imagery. Then, when a client needs to shift his emotional state, ground himself in the present, or self-soothe, in session or at home, he can call his safe place or resource imagery to mind.

Mark, a fifty-eight-year-old carpenter, started therapy with me after his wife requested a divorce and asked him to move out of their home. "I feel like such a loser," he said. "I'm depressed and embarrassed, and I hate myself. This feels just like the time my mother sent me to live with my aunt when I was five years old. Nobody really wanted me back then—not my mother and not my aunt." Though it was clear that Mark had both developmental (early neglect, abandonment, physical abuse by his mother) and recent adult traumas to address, we decided that he first needed to be able to better observe his feelings from a distance without getting swallowed up by shame and self-hatred. He identified three positive memories that we subsequently "installed": a memory of building a house, hammer in hand, feeling capable, strong, and proud; the image of his loyal childhood friends surrounding him and reminding him that he is loved; and the image of sitting on a huge boulder next to a raging river, dry and comfortable and able to observe the surroundings without any fear. After two RDI-focused sessions, he reported, "I'm feeling less vulnerable and pathetic, and I have a bit more compassion for myself. Overall, I feel more prepared to look at the childhood memories that my wife's actions seem to have triggered."

The goal in situations like this one is to ensure that you'll be able to maintain "dual attention" when you get to the actual processing of your traumatic memories. Again, maintaining dual

When traumatic memories
are properly processed,
the brain replaces old,
outdated circuits
with new, healthy circuits.

attention means that you can remain solidly and comfortably oriented and connected to your therapist and her office in the present while accessing and processing relevant traumatic memories. Here, in the preparation phase, before you jump into the deep end of the pool, your therapist wants to be sure that you can identify and tolerate feelings related to your current distress, and that you have the ability to stay within your window of tolerance at all times—grounded, present, and safe.

Your therapist will teach you to be mindful of all that is emerging emotionally and in your body. Again and again, she will ask, "What are you noticing now, and where do you feel that in your body?" When I work with new clients, I teach them to notice without judgment, and to observe with self-compassion and curiosity. I invite them to be a passenger on a train just watching the scenery go by, or to simply notice what's unfolding inside, in the same way that they might watch clouds floating along in the sky. I remind them that they don't need to get too close. Although it's important to pay attention and stay open to all that emerges, everything can remain at a safe distance.

Again, if clients come to therapy with worrisome high-risk behaviors (such as addictions, suicidality, or self-injury), or daily life instability (for example, difficulty getting to work, violence in the home, or acute medical or self-care problems), we might need to prioritize safety and functioning, taking additional stabilization measures before considering trauma-focused work. Together, we would come up with a plan to decrease distress, improve functioning and safety, and increase supports. In addition to emphasizing the importance of developing imaginal resources, I might teach my clients various coping skills (such as diaphragmatic breathing, self-hypnosis, or grounding) and engage them in some exercises focused on increasing self-compassion. Or perhaps I'd introduce some basic cognitive behavioral skills like positive self-talk or affirmations. Again, the needs of every client are going to be different, and the kinds of stabilization strategies offered by different therapists will vary greatly. These are simply examples of typical self-regulation strategies clients might use in their day-to-day life to reclaim and maintain a sense of control.

In discussing the importance of being stable "enough" before focusing on traumatic memories, I want to share some thoughts about EMDR and medication. Some of my clients are already on medications when they come into treatment. Other clients are curious about them. I often suggest that they see what we can do with EMDR therapy before considering medication to manage symptoms. My hope is that our work, whether it's skills focused, resource development, or trauma processing work, will lead to symptom reduction and to relief from depression, anxiety, fear, dissociation, and other post-traumatic stress symptoms. However, if clients are really not able to function and are not responding quickly to stabilization strategies, resourcing, or trauma processing, if they're not sleeping or eating or able to get up, get to work, or take care of their kids, I might send them for a medication evaluation.

In discussing medication, I always share some of the interesting findings from the eight-session study of EMDR and Prozac in the treatment of PTSD, mentioned earlier. The study compared the effects of EMDR therapy with standard doses of Prozac or a placebo (pill). The subjects taking the placebo did well, showing 42 percent improvement after eight weeks, and the subjects receiving Prozac did only slightly better. Those subjects receiving only EMDR therapy did much better; one in four experienced such a significant reduction in symptoms that they no longer met the criteria for a PTSD diagnosis. For those who took Prozac, only one in ten experienced this kind of reduction in symptoms. And, when subjects were taken off this medicine, of course their symptoms returned. However, when EMDR sessions were discontinued, subjects continued to get better, with symptoms showing further reductions at six- and eight-month check-ins. These results suggest that EMDR therapy can actually eliminate PTSD for good, whereas Prozac and similar medications provide only temporary symptom relief.

If I see a client who is also seeing a psychiatrist or a nurse practitioner who's prescribing medication, I always contact that medical professional. I want them to be aware of our treatment plan and understand how they can support our work. Because there may be brief periods in treatment where a client feels a little worse before they feel better or because they may have a bad week or a few hard days, I want the other professionals involved to know what to expect. I also talk with them about the goal of being able to reduce the use of medication over time as a client gets relief through EMDR therapy.

It is critical that you let your therapist know if you're taking any psychiatric medications, because some can interfere with information processing, particularly those that dampen emotional arousal and reactivity. On some medications, clients may find that they are not able to access emotion. In those cases, I may ask a prescriber if it's possible to reduce the dose of a particular medicine or if it would be okay for a client to simply refrain from taking it on the morning of a session so we are able to access a bit more emotion and body experience. There needs to be enough access and arousal to get some traction as we attempt to get the wheels of the brain's information processing system turning.

PHASE 3 — *Assessment: Activating the Memory*

Once the client can tolerate a range of emotions and maintain dual attention, it's time to begin addressing traumatic memories associated with current distress and the problems they brought to therapy. Clients are asked to self-monitor between sessions, noticing triggers, reactions, and possible associations to earlier traumatic experiences. Some therapists provide the TICES framework for tracking, asking clients to note the *triggers, images,* negative *cognitions* (thoughts), *emotions,* and physical *sensations* associated with moments of increased distress. They are then invited to share their observations at every session.

Typically, we look at the symptoms that are causing the most disruption in the client's life and work to identify earlier experiences and messages associated with those symptoms. We focus on one problem—a behavior pattern, belief, feeling, or physical symptom—at a time. If the symptom is panic when dealing with authority figures, for example, I might directly ask, "When was the earliest time in your life that you remember experiencing panic when dealing with authority figures?" That question might take a client back to an episode with a parent, teacher, coach, bully, or spouse—or to other memories related to the experience of powerlessness, fear, or a sense of feeling vulnerable or out of control. Most often, I ask my clients to "float back" with me, encouraging them to follow the current activation in their bodies back in time to explore for relevant "felt" memories. "Think about that experience from last week when you panicked with your boss. Bring up a picture of the worst moment with her, and notice the emotions and sensations, and any negative beliefs about yourself that emerge as you turn your attention to it (for example, *I'm bad, I'm vulnerable*

Memories are containers
for images, feelings,
sensations, and beliefs.

and in danger, I have no voice). Close your eyes, if you'd like, and follow that experience, in your body, back over time to the earliest time that you can remember experiencing something similar to this." We might engage in multiple "floatback" rounds, floating back further and further, taking our time to explore earlier and earlier associations. Once we have identified relevant memories, current distress triggers and symptoms, and goals for future behaviors and coping, we are ready to begin processing.

You and your therapist will decide together which "target" to begin with. Since current symptoms are related to traumatic memories that remain inadequately processed in the nervous system, therapists often will begin with the earliest or worst relevant memory. We want to address any and all problems at the foundational or root level. That said, we trust that wherever we start, other relevant memories will emerge in the course of our processing, coming to the surface as they need to get resolved. As mentioned, if a client can't identify an earlier memory or is reluctant to focus on a memory for any reason, the therapist might suggest focusing on a current trigger or symptom instead. And if a client is dealing with a recent big-*T* or little-*t* event (such as a recent car accident, public humiliation, job firing, or traumatic loss of a loved one) clearly linked to current difficulties, there is no need to float back to earlier memories. The recent traumatic event would be considered an appropriate target.

Once we decide on a particular target, which may be a past event or a current trigger, we move into the assessment phase. Here, we work to activate that target through a series of questions. These questions are informed by the Components of a Memory diagram that I shared with you in chapter 1. I might ask a client, "When you think about that assault at age fifteen, what picture represents the worst part of that memory or experience?" (If the client can't access a picture, she is encouraged to just think about the experience.) "What is the negative belief about yourself associated with that memory or that experience? If you could let go of that old belief, what would you rather believe about yourself going forward into the future?"

You and your therapist will identify a negative belief that still stirs inside you when you think about the traumatic experience, and then you will set a goal for the future, identifying a positive belief that you'd like to embrace and integrate instead. Perhaps establishing that future goal wakes up your thinking brain, readying it for the process that lies ahead.

Then, you will rate that positive belief. "On a scale from one to seven, how true does that positive belief feel right now as you think about that memory? Seven means that it feels completely true, and one means that it doesn't feel true at all." At the start of a session, the positive belief often doesn't feel very true. That positive belief might be *I'm good enough*, or, *I'm safe now*, or, *I have choices*. Very often, the positive belief is no higher than a one or two, but again, we're trying to access the part of the brain that knows there's a more adaptive or accurate perspective, even if it doesn't feel possible to entertain that perspective just yet.

Your therapist will ask you, "As you think about this incident, what are the emotions that emerge? And on a scale of zero to ten, how disturbing are those feelings? How disturbing is this memory as you connect with those emotions—ten being the worst disturbance imaginable and zero being no disturbance at all?" She is trying to get a baseline rating of your distress level before starting the processing work, so you will have a way to evaluate your progress over time.

"Target" memories are the ones that hold the trauma. They are the starting point in EMDR therapy.

Then, finally, she will ask you, "Where do you experience this distress in your body? What sensations are you aware of, and where do you experience those sensations?" I also like to inquire, when asking about bodily sensations, whether my clients are aware of any impulses or urges. "As you think about this memory and focus on the feelings, beliefs, and sensations associated with it, is there any urge to do something—to flee, to kick, to scream, to hide, to get small?" And sure enough, most people are able to identify some urge to do something that's part of that memory constellation. It often gives me a hint as to the actions that got shut down at the time of the trauma. It offers a clue that just maybe, that little kid or adult wanted to run or scream but couldn't. That urge or impulse is still trapped or locked in the nervous system and will ultimately be part of what we focus on and free up in the processing.

All of these questions serve to "activate" your target memory, helping you become aware of and in touch with its multiple components, always with one foot in the past and one in the present. Now you are ready to begin processing.

PHASE 4 — *Desensitization: Processing Memories and Current Triggers*

In the next phase, the desensitization phase, we reintroduce bilateral stimulation. As discussed earlier, it might be fingers moving back and forth in front of the client's eyes. It might involve using a light bar, tapping on clients' hands as they rest them on their laps, or having clients hold tactile pulsars that vibrate back and forth. It may also mean having the client listen to auditory stimuli through headphones.

Your therapist will remind you of the components of the memory that were identified during the assessment phase. For instance,

"Think about the image, the negative belief 'I'm not good enough,' the emotions of fear, grief, and shame, and the sensations in your stomach and your shoulders. And notice what comes. Just be a passenger on a train, watching the scenery go by." You might be reminded, "It's old stuff. You're safe now and no longer alone. It's okay to let whatever happens, happen. There is no right or wrong way to do this." As you settle in, your brain automatically begins to process the memory: the train moves down the track, dropping off what's no longer needed or true at one station, picking up what's been missing or what's important now at the next.

After about thirty to sixty seconds or a set of twenty-four to thirty back-and-forth passes of eye movements, tones, hand taps, or lights, your therapist will check in with you. "What are you noticing? What do you get now?" He may gently ask you to come back to your emotions and the sensations in your body, to come back to your senses and to stay out of your head. EMDR therapy is an experiential, body-focused approach. Clients familiar with talk therapy sometimes want to narrate or interpret what's coming up or, perhaps, get into an extended discussion. I encourage my clients to simply notice, stay with the body and their emotions, and stay with what's emerging in terms of imagery (for instance, the doctor offering the diagnosis, the look on the patient's face, the patient's daughter starting to cry) and sensory experiences (the feeling of panic and nausea, the tightening of muscles, and the impulse to run). I remind them that there will be time to reflect on it all, but first, we need to make space for all the components of the experience to emerge, be witnessed, and be processed. I tell them that all parts of themselves are welcome and are invited to share in the experience.

In this process, we often see a chronological unfolding of memory. Clients start to put together pieces of a puzzle, connect dots,

Clients are passengers on a train, watching the scenery go by. The therapist is the conductor.

and remember or understand how an experience happened in real time. Sometimes other related experiences—"feeder memories"— emerge during processing. Most of the time, I simply encourage the client to notice and continue to see what emerges or changes. Sometimes, however, I will purposely intervene to keep the processing in the present or more narrowly focused, bringing the client back to the original target again and again and limiting associations if it appears that the client isn't quite ready to safely tackle other memories or difficult emotions.

Sometimes experiences or aspects of experiences that had previously been unconscious become conscious. Some people start to get in touch with feelings or sensations for the very first time because it is finally safe enough to attend to the pain or to stop pushing away the truth of what happened. Often, as clients are taking notice of what's emerging, they arrive at new insights, new understandings, and more adult, more compassionate perspectives.

Three familiar themes emerge again and again in trauma processing. These themes relate to the concepts of (1) responsibility and defectiveness; (2) safety and vulnerability; and (3) power and control. If processing gets stuck on any of these themes, your therapist is there to help. When you are stuck on issues connected to shame and guilt, and the belief that you are at fault, you are in the domain of responsibility; here, your therapist may help you look at circumstances from a different perspective and with new information. (For example, "What if this were your best friend? What would you say to her?") When you get confused between the past and the present and struggle with the sense that you are somehow still in danger, you are in the domain of safety; here your therapist might ask you to consider all of the information that supports the idea that there is no longer a threat to your safety. ("How many years have passed since this happened? And how old are you now?") And finally, when you are feeling helpless and immobilized, you are in the domain of power and control; here, your therapist might emphasize the choices now available to you. ("If this were to happen today, what choices would you have to take care of yourself?") A client's negative belief, identified at the start of a session, often foreshadows the theme that is likely to emerge most prominently in the work.

Your therapist is also there to help you stay within your window of tolerance. Strong emotions and high levels of distress are expected and welcome, but you need to maintain a witnessing stance and dual attention—one foot in the present, one in the past; internally focused while externally grounded in the present—at all times. When necessary, I encourage my clients to slow down, take a deep breath, and orient themselves to my office. To help, I might even encourage them to stand up and toss a ball with me or push with their hands against a wall to ensure that they are fully connected to the present moment and not sliding into the past or getting too "blended" with a younger, traumatized part of themselves. I may remind the client, "You're not alone. I'm here with you this time. You're thirty-five years old. That happened a long time ago." Or, "Remember, it's just a feeling, just a sensation. It's part of an old memory. You're actually safe now."

As clients process their traumatic life experiences, it often becomes clear that many things needed to happen but didn't. Over and over, I hear about the child who was unable to call out for help, the rape victim who wanted to run, the teen who wanted to fight back when being bullied. But for all the obvious reasons, they couldn't. Then there are the stories of being alone and frightened and confused when no one noticed and came to the rescue.

No one showed up to protect, explain, validate, reassure, or soothe. As I'm facilitating a client's processing, I'm listening and looking for opportunities to help the client with completion, repair, and closure.

Remember when we were kids and somebody would shout, "Do-over!" when something didn't turn out or come out right? In EMDR therapy, we invite clients to consider what a "do-over" would look like or sound like. Sometimes these reparative scenes emerge spontaneously. For example, while tracking the bilateral stimulation, clients see themselves beating the crap out of their perpetrator or fleeing from a life-threatening situation. They imagine entering a scene as their current adult self to comfort and rescue their hurt child self. They offer up an end to their story that represents justice, revenge, triumph, or an appropriate intervention on the part of others: parents, teachers, or other helpers. If these do-overs don't emerge spontaneously, the therapist might intervene and offer encouragement (emphasizing choices), ask pointed questions, or put forward certain suggestions. "If you could have fought back, what would it have looked like?" "If you could have spoken up, what would you have wanted to say?" "What did that little kid need in that moment? Imagine bringing that to her." Whatever emerges, the therapist says to the client, "Go with that. Stay with that." And processing continues with bilateral stimulation, integrating that possibility, that imagined scene, or that conversation, eventually transforming the memory being held in the nervous system.

The first step in processing is to make our way through the actual experiences, desensitizing the fear in the body, and processing the other critical emotions—the grief, anger, unmet longing, shame, and guilt. But often, particularly when dealing with complex trauma, there is more to the work. Here, the goal is also to help clients reach a place where they can imagine saying what they couldn't say back then ("I hate you," "Get away from me") and doing what they couldn't do back then (run, fight, speak up). There is often a need for the adult self to engage with the child or younger self in a way that offers a course correction ("It wasn't your fault," "They were wrong—you *are* lovable," "You're not alone anymore").

Chantel is a thirty-five-year-old graduate student who sought treatment to deal with post-traumatic stress symptoms related to multiple sexual abuse encounters with her mother's boyfriend between the ages of six and twelve. In one of her most powerful sessions, reflecting the culmination of many weeks of work, Chantel processed the terror, grief, and shame associated with one of the most humiliating and violent encounters with this man. She moved from seeing her "younger self" as weak and disgusting to recognizing her as brave and resourceful. She was able to "rescue" her from the past, bringing her into her "safe place" in the present where she comforted her and acknowledged what had happened. Over and over, she quietly whispered to her younger self, "It wasn't your fault." After spending a total of four months processing her worst sexual abuse memories, Chantel reported, "I'm no longer getting flooded by images of that evil man. I've ejected him from my brain, and the nightmares and flashbacks have completely stopped. And I really know now that I wasn't responsible for the abuse; I was a victim and truly did the best I could under the circumstances."

Despite this amazing progress, Chantel continued to avoid interactions with others whenever she felt that there was the possibility of conflict, and she struggled to speak up for herself when others were hurtful toward her. Interestingly, in her EMDR

The "do-over" empowers people to imagine defending themselves, speaking their minds, or righting a wrong.

sessions, she had been unable to directly express her anger toward her perpetrator until something in her adult life made it possible for her to access a deep sense of righteous indignation. In hearing about a case of blatant police brutality, Chantel felt the rage that she had never let herself feel toward her abuser. We decided to target a scene that she had watched on the evening news twenty-four hours earlier. Chantel, a Black woman, had watched in total horror and disbelief a scene involving a white officer beating an unarmed Black teenager. While engaged in EMDR processing, she accessed and expressed her rage toward the police officer, but then, within one set of bilateral stimulation, spontaneously shifted and started to direct this rage at her mother's boyfriend. I encouraged her to continue until she felt satisfied that she had said and done everything she needed to say and do. I asked her, "What would justice look like?" and encouraged her to continue processing. She chose not to tell me what she said and did to him in her mind's eye, but at the end of the session, she said, "I'm finally truly free from him. I'm ready to reclaim my voice and my power." With this final piece of work, Chantel began to express her needs in relationships with others and stopped shying away from potential conflicts. She was no longer afraid to speak truth to power and declared that she was ready to move on to the next chapter of her life. With that, we began to explore what that next chapter might include.

So, there are often several levels to the work. There's the desensitization aspect, decreasing the distress, and putting the past back into the past; seizing the opportunity to say or do what couldn't be said or done at the time; and remobilizing one's body, reclaiming one's voice, and aiming for full expression and closure. Clients are able to return to the present, knowing that the trauma is truly over and that it wasn't their fault, that they did the best they could, and that they deserve to heal and thrive. And then, there's the developmental repair aspect. This aspect of the work is about making sure that there is now self-compassion and validation where previously there had been none, and creating opportunities for child parts of self to be heard and cared for when, previously, there had only been criticism, neglect, and hurt. Connecting the adult self with the child self or selves in imagination is a chance for adult clients to recognize their unmet needs, vulnerabilities, and longings. The work often leads to recognition of parts of themselves who have felt invisible, misunderstood, or not good enough. It's an opportunity to step in and bring much-needed empathy and nurturance to those parts of themselves. You will continue to process—with sets of bilateral stimulation, noticing what emerges, staying engaged with the experience, and checking in with your therapist along the way—until your distress level lowers to a one or a zero.

PHASE 5 — *Installation: Integrating a New, More Positive Perspective*

At this point, you're ready to move on to the installation phase, where you're asked to bring up the positive belief that you identified at the start of the session, such as *I am good enough, I'm safe now,* or *I have choices.* Sometimes, you'll discover that the words of the original positive belief have evolved and that now, another statement fits even better. Once you decide on the most fitting positive belief, your therapist will ask you to rate how true this belief feels. For example, "As you think about that original experience, on a scale of one (not true) to seven (totally true), how true do the words *I'm good enough* feel to you now?"

You'll then continue processing with sets of bilateral stimulation until the validity of that positive belief reaches seven—a point

EMDR therapy allows you to transform old, well-worn, negative beliefs into new, updated, and more positive ones.

where you can fully and genuinely endorse this new belief even while thinking about the bad things that previously happened to you. Ideally, the new belief now feels true, heart and soul, through and through. At the end of the session in which she was finally able to express her rage, my client Chantel's positive belief was *I am powerful and can take care of myself.* She smiled from ear to ear and said that it was a seven and felt totally true. She was sitting up straight in her chair, making strong eye contact, and looking *fully* alive and triumphant.

If there are blocks to fully integrating the positive belief, your therapist will likely ask, "What might be keeping it from being a seven?" Often, I discover that a *but* or a *what-if* is holding my client back. "But what if other people still think it's my fault?" Or, "What if I make a mistake like that again?" Sometimes, old messages return to interfere with the integration of new, more adaptive beliefs. For example, as a client focuses on the words *I am strong and can do anything,* perhaps she hears her critical mother's voice in her mind saying, "Now, don't get too full of yourself." If material like this emerges, I might remind the client that this is old stuff, too, and that she should just let it go by. I might also ask her if she would ever dream of saying such a thing to her own daughter. Of course the answer is a resounding "No!" In considering this and continuing to process, I would expect to see movement toward a seven, signaling the full integration of the positive belief.

PHASE 6 — *Body Scan: Checking In with the Body*

In EMDR therapy, we always come back to the body to check our work. So in the body scan phase, after completing the "installation" of a new positive belief, your therapist will ask you to think about the target again—the original incident or trauma-related trigger—along with the positive belief, noticing how your body feels upon reaching that point in the process. The target may have dramatically changed in your mind. Ideally, it feels and looks different. When you think about the original incident while holding your new positive belief in mind, and scan your body for any residual distress, you might still notice some uncomfortable sensations, perhaps some tension or a feeling in your stomach or a slight headache. If so, your therapist will ask you to focus on the sensation(s) and continue with additional sets of bilateral stimulation, checking in after each set until you are able to report that your body feels clear, calm, and grounded, with no obvious disturbance.

PHASE 7 — *Closure: Putting Stuff Away and Preparing to Leave*

Every session ends with the closure phase, whether the work is complete (distress = zero or one, validity of the positive belief = seven) or not. Closure is all about making sure you are fully present and ready to go back out into your world, ready to function at your best. If you and your therapist manage to complete all relevant phases during your session and you are in a positive frame of mind, you may not need to do much in terms of closure other than taking some time to reflect on your work with your therapist. I typically ask, "What feels like the most important thing that you learned today about yourself? What was it like for you to experience this? What was it like to do this work with me?"

Sometimes the session needs to be brought to a close while a client is still working to desensitize a past trauma or a trigger. If the processing remains incomplete and there is still some degree of distress, your therapist will most likely engage you in some kind of formal closure exercise. I often have my clients put their traumatic material away in an imaginary "container" or have them return to their "safe place." I might encourage those who have a dissociative disorder to check inside to make sure that all the parts of their internal system feel settled enough and able to transition back out into the world.

PHASE 8 — *Reevaluation: Assessing Progress and Reengaging*

Each new session begins with a reevaluation phase. Your therapist will start by asking you about all that has transpired since your last session together. She might ask, "How did your week go? What did you notice that was relevant to the work that we did together? What's changed with regard to your symptoms? How are you sleeping? Any dreams or nightmares?" Then she will reevaluate the target you worked on in the previous session, asking, "What picture represents the worst part of that memory or trigger situation now?" It's not unusual to discover that the worst part is different from what it was in an earlier session. Whatever the case, the target is reevaluated and, if there is still distress associated with it, the work continues, picking up the processing where it left off in the previous session. If you and your therapist discover that the work is truly complete (no distress, strong positive belief about yourself, clear body scan), you might decide to turn to other related targets from the past or triggers from the present. Or perhaps you'll decide to move into the future to look at goals that you want to address. Maybe you'll choose to work on another aspect of your life. If that's the case, the two of you would return to history taking to explore further and to design a treatment plan for the next identified problem area.

PAST, PRESENT, AND FUTURE

Once relevant past experiences and present triggers have been addressed, you will be invited to imagine yourself in the future, effectively dealing with a challenging situation and feeling a sense of triumph and mastery. If you can imagine that future scene (often referred to as a "future template") with confidence, your therapist will add bilateral stimulation to help integrate and strengthen this new sense of yourself. Eventually, you'll be encouraged to turn that scene into an imaginary movie in your head, with a beginning, middle, and end. If you get stuck or run into difficulties at any point, your therapist will help you problem-solve to move past them. When you are finally able to imagine yourself coping effectively throughout the movie, your therapist will add bilateral stimulation once again.

Remember Mark, the carpenter whose wife filed for divorce and asked him to leave their home? After processing his childhood traumatic memories and several incidents from his troubled marriage and subsequent divorce, he came to realize that his wife had likely had an affair while they were married. He came to understand his own denial about the affair and looked compassionately at the reasons why he had chosen to "look the other way." To make a long story short, it had everything to do with his history of childhood neglect. As he held in mind the positive beliefs that had come out of his processing sessions—*I am lovable* and *I deserve respect and honesty*—he successfully imagined a future movie in which he confronted his ex-wife about her infidelity. At the following session, he reported that he had actually called his ex-wife to follow through with that conversation. All in all, he thought it had gone well, and said, "I'm actually really proud of myself. I said what I needed to say, just like we practiced it in our EMDR session, and then I said goodbye. I feel like a weight has been lifted off my shoulders."

At points like this in my work with clients, we often slow down and take some time to celebrate all that has been accomplished. We also get excited about all that lies ahead. I have been known to shed a few tears as I witness the emergence of clients' strength, clarity, and self-respect. It is often quite inspiring.

Michael: When I first heard about EMDR therapy, in Dr. Magnavita's office, I was skeptical and a little scared. It sounded nothing like any other therapy I'd experienced. But once I began the treatment, I found it extraordinary. It allowed me to "float back" to precise moments in time, precise environments I had grown up in, and precise feelings and sensations frozen inside me that I hadn't ever known were there.

Our sessions would typically start with a discussion about what was going on with me and how I had been feeling since my previous visit. Often, we'd talk about a nightmare I'd had the night before. When the time came for processing, Dr. Magnavita would ask me to focus on one of my traumatic memories, a recent trigger situation, or a current symptom, like the nightmare. He'd ask me several questions to help activate the target and would then tell me to follow his fingers as he waved them back and forth. "Just let it come," he would say. "Don't try to figure it out; it will all sort itself out."

I got to know, for myself, the phenomenon of reexperiencing emotions and sensations that had been perfectly preserved for decades in my brain and *body*.

In one early session, I was able to see the room in our home in Denver where my crib was, the door slightly open and the light coming in. I experienced the feeling of panic that I had had in that crib when I realized that I was alone and nobody was coming. I was so hungry that my stomach ached. Sitting there in Dr. Magnavita's office, I felt a deep sense of sorrow and compassion for that child who was feeling so distraught and totally abandoned.

I came to have a deep understanding for the first time in my life of how neglected I had actually been.

After processing that deep, preverbal trauma, I felt lighter and safer than I had ever felt before. It gave me the encouragement to keep coming back week after week to address my other symptoms.

To relieve my panic around women, we targeted trigger situations where I fled from moments of potential intimacy with women—and what immediately came up as I started to process was the recurring memory of my mother bathing me. Only this time it was filled in—all the sensations, all the feelings, all the images. And, for the first time, I was fully aware of the extreme terror and paralysis that accompanied that six-year-old's experience in the bathtub.

Dr. Magnavita encouraged me to "just notice, just observe" and to refrain from jumping to any conclusions. At points, he gently said, as he had before, "Take my hand," to reassure me that I wasn't alone and that he was there with me.

I was able to access the intense panic that accompanied the uncomfortably pleasurable sensation of my mother washing my genitals. At six years old I most definitely didn't want her doing that to me, but I was frozen, I couldn't flee or push her away or protest; I had to just let it happen, screaming as loud as I could—but only in my mind—for it to stop.

After the session, I honestly did not know what to make of the high level of terror associated with this memory. I questioned whether my mother, with her poor boundaries and flirtatious,

Recurring disturbing dreams are often the brain's attempt to resolve traumatic memories.

sexualized style of relating, had actually molested me, but I wasn't able to come to any conclusions. What I did know was that millions of parents innocently bathe their children without creating an indelibly traumatic memory, so I had to have been responding to something, some other cue from her that overwhelmed my nervous system. As it turned out, it wasn't until later in my treatment, when other aspects of my trauma history eventually emerged, that I was actually able to make sense of what had happened on that day.

Over the course of several sessions, I continued to process the traumatic episode in the bathtub. I came to realize that I didn't protest because I was terrified of being abandoned. I came to understand, even without having answers to all my questions, that my body froze because my brain perceived danger and because I felt like I had no choice or sense of control in that moment. In processing the memory, I went through several intense emotional stages—first disbelief, then sadness, then anger, then profound grief. Because of the lack of safety and predictability in my childhood and the unprocessed terror that my body carried over the years, I wound up paying a high price in my adult years. I felt a sense of deep regret, though I landed in a place of genuine self-compassion.

Those were raw, intensely emotional days. Though the work was challenging, each day I felt a little better—like I could finally breathe.

We then worked to process my most pervasive traumas—being beaten up by my brother, my father, and the bully at school; the constant fear; and the devastating, chronic experiences of neglect.

Little by little, month by month, my life was improving. I had steady, fulfilling work again. I had furnished my apartment and was cooking and caring for myself. I stopped staying out late at night and drinking excessively. My constant anxiety was gone. I was no longer haunted by the memory of my mother giving me a bath. But I still had the nightmares and the fear of bathrooms and heights.

It wasn't until late in my treatment that my brain was finally ready to work on those fears. Floating back from the nightmare in which I was an accomplice to a murder and the police arrested me and put me in prison, I was suddenly *not in a prison* but in a doctor's office at age six. Alone in the exam room, I was lying face down on the table, naked under a hospital gown. I heard the door shut. I could see the pale green and white speckled pattern of the linoleum floor. I remembered the doctor's white coat and his voice. And then I heard the sound of his belt buckle hitting the floor and reexperienced the excruciating pain of being raped.

I had finally discovered what being put in prison in my recurring nightmare was about—and why I was terrified of bathroom stalls. The prison was my doctor's office. I was scared to death I would be taken back to that office again. I finally understood *why* the thought of walking into a stall in a public bathroom, pulling my pants down, and being totally exposed created such anxiety in me: it was a *trigger* for that trauma—a hyperlink—that transported me right back to that traumatic experience; the boy in me was convinced that if I was that exposed, that doctor would climb over the stall and rape me again. My body held that terror, even though my mind didn't know yet what it was connected to.

In talking with Dr. Magnavita and later with Debbie, I also came to understand why the episode in the bathtub with my mother was so radioactively charged for me. As best as I can reconstruct, the interaction with my mother in the bathtub occurred shortly after the molestation incident with the doctor. Without any *conscious* recall of the rape, the experience with my mother seemed to have

Triggers are like hyperlinks—instantly transporting you back to when the trauma first occurred.

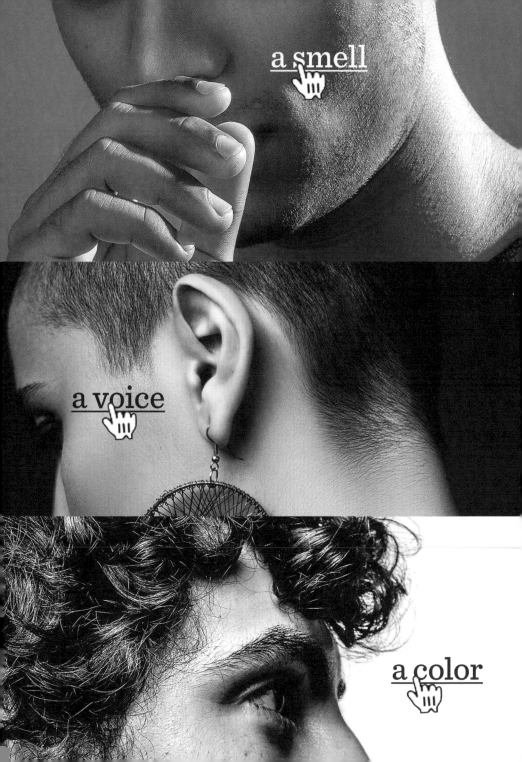

a smell

a voice

a color

triggered the terror associated with that event. The situation with my mother shared features with the situation with the doctor—I was alone with a powerful adult, I was dependent on that adult, I was naked, and my body was being touched in a way that made me uncomfortable. So I panicked and my body froze, just like it did with the doctor; I expected to be violated again. And just as I stared at the linoleum floor in the doctor's office, so, with my mother, I fixated on the drops of water from the washcloth hitting the water in the bathtub, helping me to psychologically escape from the terror of the moment. Over time, just as my mother's touch came to be associated with the rape by the doctor, any suggestion of physical intimacy with a woman, or the simple act of entering a public bathroom, came to be associated with those buried memories, triggering the impulse to either flee or shut down. I didn't choose to make these associations. My brain made these connections a long time ago ("neurons that fire together wire together"), without my mind ever knowing.

The Empire State Building nightmare—in which I dreamt that I'd fallen from the top to the pavement below—was also a buoy, tethered to buried trauma. Floating back from my fear of crossing a bridge, I remembered hanging from a swing set at age five as my older sister continued to tickle and torment me even though I begged her to stop. I felt terror—I was not going to be able to hold on—and finally, I had to let go. I fell, landed on my arm, and broke it. I realized that *that's* what my nightmare had always been about; landing on the street beneath the Empire State Building was actually me landing in the dirt, on my arm, in the backyard of our home in Diablo, California.

Both recurring nightmares—being put in prison and falling from the Empire State Building—were my mind, caught in a repeating loop, trying to tell me a story, trying to let me know that there were forgotten parts of me that needed attention and healing.

But the realization that possibly had the greatest effect on me was that the paralyzed state I found myself in after losing my job at Ogilvy & Mather mirrored the same frozen state that I was in during the bathtub episode with my mother and in the doctor's office—*I couldn't move.* Immobilized by a terror that actually came from my older, unprocessed traumatic memories, I once again felt powerless and panic-stricken, plunged into an adult echo of that same childhood paralysis. I had tried so hard for so long to escape my trauma, but in the end, I was right back there, right back where it had all begun.

In the course of my EMDR work, I came to realize that I was no longer a child with a child's minimal tools for coping. As an adult, I could go back and give the parts of me who were frozen in fear, who were bullied, who were raped, and who were broken and neglected, the love and attention and kindness they deserved. I could bring an arsenal of healthy offerings to these boys, these parts of me, responding to them as the parent they never had.

Survivors can often keep memories and symptoms at bay until the tolerable becomes intolerable.

5

Contemplating Treatment: Am I Ready? Can I Really Do This?

Michael: I've become such a strong advocate for EMDR because I've experienced the rewards, but I remember the questions and concerns I had when I started: What if I can't do this? What if I feel too much—or too little? What if I black out? I pushed through because my need for healing was stronger than my fears. I was tired of feeling like everyone else was living on the other side of a window. I couldn't access that other reality no matter how hard I tried. I wanted in. And I definitely wanted *out* of my ongoing state of misery.

Debbie: These are some of the questions that I hear from clients in first sessions or on the phone before we meet in person, and these are the answers I give. Every therapist has their own style and will answer these questions differently. You need to pay attention only to whether their answers help you feel comfortable and safe with them and whether the game plan being proposed makes sense to you.

In these early interactions, I begin to get clues about the fears and concerns that clients have about committing to a trauma-focused psychotherapy. Clients' answers to these questions also give me a sense of their interpersonal styles and help me anticipate what they might need from me to feel comfortable and secure in therapy. Finally, they highlight where there might be misinformation or myths about EMDR therapy or trauma treatment in general that I will need to address early in our time together.

Will I have to relive anything? The work will involve identifying memories and getting in touch with the imagery, feelings, sensations, and thoughts connected to actual adverse life experiences. But we will be doing this in a way that will allow you to feel securely grounded, present, and safe at all times. We will always work at a pace that assures that you will not find yourself overwhelmed, dysregulated, or disoriented. We'll always keep you within your window of tolerance; that is a top priority. Our goal is to always be working within that optimal zone of arousal for processing, in which there's enough emotion and connection to your body to get things moving, but not so much that you are overwhelmed and have to resort to familiar defensive maneuvers.

This work is much more about redoing than reliving. It's about accessing the memories and working with the feelings, thoughts, and sensations within a safe environment and with a compassionate, trustworthy person, allowing you to experience and make sense of it all in a way that just wasn't possible at an earlier time in your life.

I want you to feel safe and secure from the get-go, so over and over, I'll continue to remind you that "I'm not going to let you drown. I'm not going to leave your side for a moment. We're going to go as slowly as the slowest part of you needs to go. That said, if and when you're ready and you give me the signal, we'll go as fast as you're ready to go, so you can get the heck out of the past and

As you approach your memories, your therapist will set a safe pace so you don't get in over your head.

get on with your life in the present. You're in control. I'll always be here to help you witness and observe from a distance."

Will I have to relive *everything*? You will not have to process every traumatic experience that you've had in your life, or even every memory related to the events that specifically led you to seek treatment. (Hallelujah!) What we'll do is choose representative experiences, linked to certain symptoms, beliefs, or themes. And in working on those, we will look for shifts in your nervous system and thinking. Often, when you experience shifts related to one memory or symptom, shifts in other memories and symptoms naturally follow. And with those shifts comes relief. Often, change generalizes across memories and symptoms from session to session without any additional work between sessions, simply with the passage of time. As new, adult perspectives are integrated, old experiences are regarded differently. Perceptions about yourself and the world around you in the present spontaneously start to change.

What if I don't remember? We tend to think of memory as a story or narrative, or as a visual image, but sometimes memory takes other forms. It's expressed as a sensation in the body, a physical awareness or bodily knowing. Eugene Gendlin, a well-known philosopher and psychologist, coined a term for this: he referred to one's "felt sense." *I feel sick to my stomach and there's a sense of danger. I feel frightened, small, trapped, and unable to move. I somehow know that this is connected to the abuse by my brother.* Particularly when we're dealing with very early, preverbal memories, it's all in the body. Memory is somatically based and often experienced as motor patterns, impulses, or physical sensations. Your mind may not remember but your body does.

EMDR therapists continually observe and evaluate how the body responds to, defends against, and processes trauma at a sensorimotor (body and movement) level. Often when we explore the past based on current symptoms or triggers, clients remember a feeling, a sensation, or an experience, often without details or a full narrative. Sometimes, memories that were previously unconscious or out of awareness do emerge, as a story, as an image, or just as a felt sense. That said, it's okay if you don't remember details or don't have a complete story—we'll work with whatever emerges moment to moment as we bring our attention to whatever is bothering you.

What if I don't want to remember or don't want to connect with painful feelings? You needed to tuck those memories far away in order to survive and create a life for yourself. But if you want to heal, it's time to retrieve them from that soundproof, emotion-proof compartment. I can assure you that you will be well prepared for this work; we won't move into processing the worst of your memories until you are totally ready. And just a reminder: You're not going to have to do this by yourself, and you're not five years old anymore. You're not fifteen years old anymore. You're now an adult with choices, and there is a real opportunity here for you to reclaim your life.

How do I know I'm not making up these memories? We are going to engage in a process together, and over the course of the process, you will arrive at your own very personal truth. If you're having a range of symptoms that somehow seem related, there is likely an underlying story waiting to be pieced together. There's a narrative that will ultimately serve to connect them all. And it's critical that we pay attention when your body speaks. As fragments of memories initially emerge as feelings, images, or a bodily felt sense, you do not need to be overly concerned with determining whether they represent objective truth. Over time, we will reflect on your memories and on how you choose to understand them. We will work together to place them within the context of your whole life.

Do I have to talk about it? Yes and no. We're probably going to need to talk about it, at least some of the time, but again, we're going to take it very slowly. We're going to find the pace that's right for you, for every part of you. Fortunately, EMDR therapy doesn't require you to describe anything in detail. It's possible to heal without a lot of words. In fact, at times you may have few or no words, and that's totally fine. We'll listen to your body and to what your emotions are telling us. We'll quietly make room for all parts of you and for your story to unfold, and over time, you'll get to a place where you can speak about it in here and eventually with others, if that's important to you. A clear goal of treatment is to help you get to a place where you can express in words precisely what you've been feeling and experiencing.

There will be no judgment. We will approach this from a place of curiosity, interest, and compassion.

What if I can't tolerate the treatment? What if I dissociate? Part of what we'll be doing at the start of treatment is making sure you have the skills and internal resources needed to stay present and connected to me. I'm going to be your guide, your partner in this work. And we're going to go moment to moment together, step by step.

This work is not therapeutic if you're outside your window of tolerance—emotionally overwhelmed, disconnected from your body or your feelings, or maybe even looking at what's going on from the ceiling. You have to be present and able to access your relevant experiences to achieve some sense of resolution. So first, we'll work on the skills and capacities that enable you to stay present. It will be just like learning anything new, developing any kind of novel skill; there will be a learning curve. And we'll attend to the parts of you that are worried about feeling overwhelmed, on alert for any signs that it's "too much." We'll make sure we have a plan that feels acceptable and well paced, and we'll work in increments. You'll be surprised to discover how you develop more and more emotional muscle, confidence, and courage over time.

IN PURSUIT OF HEALING: WHY ANY OLD THERAPIST WON'T DO

Many of my clients report that they have sought therapy in the past with little success in finding relief. Many have been in supportive talk therapy. Some report that they have focused on learning skills in various cognitive-behavioral treatments. Almost everyone who has sought treatment from multiple therapists over time describes the same phenomenon as that depicted in the Indian parable of the blind men and the elephant. Each blind man is touching a part of the elephant—one touching the tusk, one the trunk, one the side—and each is coming away with a partial and therefore distorted idea of what the whole might be. One psychiatrist might see the depression and prescribe an antidepressant medication, one might see the anxiety and prescribe a beta-blocker, one might see the phobia and suggest cognitive-behavioral therapy, one might see the relational problems and suggest couples' therapy. But they

Unfortunately, many clinicians miss the unifying theme of trauma across seemingly unrelated symptoms.

each pursue only one part of the whole. Symptoms of C-PTSD or dissociative disorders can mimic symptoms associated with other disorders. Many of my clients report being treated, previously, for numerous other disorders with poor outcomes and relatively no reprieve from their distress. Unless you can step back and see how all the parts are, in fact, directly or indirectly related to traumatic memories stored in the nervous system, or adaptations a person has made in light of traumatic experiences, you're potentially just treating all these independent components without healing the root cause. Now, that is not an economical, efficient, or particularly productive approach.

Frequently my clients report experiences with therapies where the emphasis was solely on managing symptoms. Some have managed to get to a place where the acuity of their symptoms has lessened—they are, perhaps, less depressed or anxious and better able to manage their PTSD symptoms, addictive behaviors, or compulsive efforts to avoid pain—but they are still just barely surviving. They report feeling fragile or out of control; they are certainly not happy. And they are certainly not thriving or living a full, socially connected, joyous life. Weeds keep popping up in their garden, and despite their efforts to cut them back again and again, they continue to reappear, sometimes stronger, sometimes wilder than ever before. The problem is that they are focusing on trimming them back, when pulling them out by the roots and planting something new is what's required.

Trauma survivors, with their finely tuned dissociative capacities, are actually quite skilled at keeping the trauma hidden from themselves, the people close to them, and the rest of the world. Unless a therapist asks the right questions in a moment when there is enough trust in that therapist, the details and relevance of the client's traumatic past can and will be missed. Worse, the therapist can wind up unwittingly colluding with the client's avoidance and denial, letting the therapy meander in a direction that does not lead to transformation or relief.

COMMON FEARS THAT MIGHT SLOW YOU DOWN

People report a range of fears about seeking and starting therapy and then, about actually digging into the process. First, there's the fear of trusting and becoming attached to a therapist. Clients, consciously or unconsciously, may expect to be misunderstood, shamed, or invalidated. It's not uncommon to hear, "I'm afraid to get close to anyone. Intimate relationships feel scary to me." Again, if depending on other people has never been a safe or reliable survival strategy, a phobic reaction to closeness makes total sense. Remember our ancestors' poisonous red berry!

Second, before even establishing a new therapy relationship, many survivors are already anxious about somehow screwing it up. They fear feeling vulnerable, becoming dependent, and then, ultimately being abandoned. People come into treatment believing, *If I am vulnerable and dare to trust, I'll become too dependent and needy. I'll be a burden and ultimately too much for you to handle.* Or, *If I let myself get close to you and you really get to know me, you'll surely want to get rid of me.*

Third, people often are afraid of attending to their inner experiences—everything their brains have been working endlessly to keep at bay, sometimes for years or even decades: images, thoughts, feelings, needs, sensations, impulses, and memories. They often have an overwhelming fear of emotional pain. People will say to me, "If I start to remember and feel, I will get swallowed up by negative, painful emotions. I won't be able to function." "I am terrified of what I might remember." "I'm afraid that I'll start crying and never be able to stop." "The shame and self-hatred are unbearable. I don't know that I can talk about this with anyone. It will kill me." They worry that the things that they feel or hear or think inside will indeed confirm that they are "crazy" or so "broken" that they are unable to heal.

Furthermore, clients who report more extensive dissociative symptoms may feel quite fragmented inside, with parts that hold extreme feelings and impulses (rage and violent impulses, despair and self-destructive impulses, fear and the impulse to withdraw). It's also not uncommon for there to be significant conflicts between individual parts, each part representing a different survival strategy—fight, flee, freeze, submit, or try to appease; self-attack or self-criticize; cry out or hold on for dear life. As such, there may be considerable fears related to connecting with certain dissociated parts or aspects of their personality. If parts of the person got pushed out of consciousness—banished to one of the rooms in the house, locked behind a steel door because of the memories, feelings, or impulses that they held—the idea of turning any attention toward those parts may feel terrifying. Many clients are able to share their sense of other parts (sometimes experienced as a feeling, impulse, or voice inside) quite readily at the start of treatment, whereas others need to take their time in sharing even the smallest bits of information about their "internal family." There can be traumatized child parts who may not be oriented to current time, angry parts, and suicidal parts, parts who have carried the fragments of a person's trauma story for a lifetime, and then parts who have worked diligently to make sure certain stories never get remembered or spoken out loud. People will say to me, "I'm afraid of that rageful part—that voice harasses me day and night," or, "I hate that vulnerable, needy part of me."

And, of course, there is the fear of change and the fear of failure. Even if their lives are miserable, clients may be reluctant to rock the boat; what is known is better than what is unknown. *I'm miserable, but I'm safe in my isolation. If I leave my cocoon, I'll get hurt, or I'll fail and become more depressed.* Many clients have a harsh inner critic who consistently predicts disaster or some degree of failure: *I'm just not good at therapy. I've tried it in the past, and I don't think there's any hope for me.*

Rounding out this list is the fear of disclosing. Clients often say, perhaps speaking from their youngest, most vulnerable parts, that they don't want to be disloyal to their parents, family members, or community. *If I speak up and acknowledge the truth, I'll be banished, hurt, or blamed. I was always told that whatever happens in our family stays within our family.* They feel frozen expressing genuine emotions and opinions for fear of punishment, judgment, or potential loss of attachment figures. A client of mine who escaped from an abusive religious cult would say, "I know I am speaking my truth, but a part of me feels like I'm evil for uttering even a single word. I'm terrified that somehow, they will know and then it will be over. They'll come for me."

It takes incredible courage to acknowledge that you are, in fact, in need of help, and then an even bigger dose of courage to take those first steps toward initiating psychotherapy. And what seems fairly simple and straightforward in the beginning, may turn out to be a bit more challenging than you expected. Sadly, one of the greatest casualties of trauma, particularly prolonged or repeated trauma that started in childhood, is the damage caused to your attachment system. This system, at its best, allows you to connect

and feel safe, comfortable, and regulated in intimate relationships. When complex relational trauma has left you feeling fearful
or unsure of yourself in relationships, choosing to trust someone
through thick and thin, week after week, can be extremely difficult . . . and confusing. (*Am I too dependent? Am I demanding too
much? Does my therapist really care about me, or is she just doing
her job? Will she give up on me? Is she getting a little too close?*)

When your emotional and relational operating systems are
damaged and not functioning well, therapy itself—your relationship with your psychotherapist—can potentially feel triggering or
dysregulating. That said, you will need to find a way to trust a
therapist as well as others who can help you mend your wounds.
You can't do it alone. So I want to end this chapter with a brief
discussion of attachment "styles." The more you understand your
attachment or relational style and the strategies that you have
come to use for regulating emotion while in connection with
others, the better you will do in recovery. I urge you to own your
attachment style without shame or apology—with compassion for
yourself. Talk explicitly with your therapist about the goal of trusting more, sharing more, and ultimately, feeling more secure in the
therapeutic relationship. As you learn firsthand about your attachment style in therapy, you will come to understand more about
your relational and emotional dynamics outside therapy.

UNDERSTANDING YOUR ATTACHMENT STYLE

Attachment theory, developed in the 1950s by psychologist John
Bowlby, attempts to describe how our earliest environments and
relationships either support an internalized sense of security or
disrupt our ability to connect with and trust in others. As discussed

earlier, under the best of circumstances, attachment is defined as the secure bond, established between a caregiver and infant, that sets the stage for a life of healthy relationships. Parents or caregivers who are consistently available and responsive to the needs of their infant or child—kind, attuned, interested, playful, and loving—offer a secure base from which the child can explore the world around them, take risks, and then safely return home. Securely attached infants and children can rely on their caregivers for consistent help with emotional distress; responsive adults help them stay regulated when there are "big" feelings or changes to deal with.

People who experience secure attachments early in life typically grow up to be adults capable of forming healthy and secure relationships. They tend to be relatively sure of themselves, able to self-regulate and tolerate distress, but also able to reach out and rely on others for comfort when appropriate. They trust that if and when there is a rupture in a relationship, there is indeed an opportunity for repair and reconnection, each and every time. We refer to this resilient style of relating as "secure" attachment.

When caregivers are impaired, neglectful, abusive, anxious, narcissistic or uninterested, and generally unresponsive or unavailable, it leads to significant insecurity. Infants and children learn that they cannot turn to caregivers for comfort or protection. They do not receive any soothing when they are overwhelmed or scared and thus do not learn how to self-regulate. Clients with challenging histories, reporting significant early trauma, typically grow up to have "insecure" attachment styles, with less than optimal strategies for relating and regulating within intimate relationships. Attachment researchers have identified three different insecure attachment styles that remain pretty consistent from childhood into adulthood.

In the therapeutic process, daring to trust requires courage and a huge leap of faith.

- **Insecure Anxious/Preoccupied**—Adults with this attachment style tend to be anxious, demanding, and clingy in their interactions with others. They are often intensely preoccupied with getting their needs met by a partner, friend, or professional, and overly concerned about abandonment. They have a hard time regulating their emotions and often look to others to make things better. It's not uncommon for those with an anxious/preoccupied style to choose partners without appropriate reflection and evaluation, unable to discern who might actually be able to meet their needs.

- **Insecure Avoidant/Dismissive**—Those with this attachment style tend to avoid closeness with others in an effort to protect themselves from hurt or rejection. They are typically excessively self-reliant and often quite dismissive of their own emotions as well as the emotions and needs of others, including intimate partners. They often appear distant and hard to reach because they have erected walls to protect themselves from genuine emotional engagement with others.

- **Insecure Disorganized**—Adults with this attachment style often have significant histories of severe maltreatment. As such, it is also the style most often associated with dissociative disorders. It develops when a child simultaneously needs and fears her parent or caregiver. Disorganized adults can present as chaotic, impulsive, and sometimes aggressive; different parts implement different strategies to survive, regulate, or get their needs met. As such, their behavior can appear disorganized and contradictory, seeking closeness one moment, and pushing comfort or interest away in the next. In this way the chaos of their adult relationships often mimics the toxicity and dynamics of their abusive childhood relationships.

So again, why is it important for you to reflect on your own attachment style before embarking on your first or next therapy experience? Well, the natural demands of therapy—increased vulnerability, openness to emotional experience, the need to trust and rely on another human being—will likely challenge your attachment style. You and your therapist will have to learn how to dance together, finding the right tempo and speed, communicating when something doesn't feel quite right, and making corrections and repairs when things are off course. The more you know about your own attachment style, the clearer you can be with your therapist from the outset about what's hard for you, unfamiliar to you, or confusing for you. The ultimate goal is to increase your capacity for secure attachment, both with your therapist and in your life.

But again, there's no need to figure all of this out ahead of time. A skilled therapist can help you understand more about your attachment style and will offer plenty of guidance about how to proceed.

The relationships we had with our caregivers serve as templates for our adult lives.

6

Keeping Your Eye on the Prize:
The Promise of Transformation

Michael: If you were to ask me, "What is the most important return on the investment of EMDR therapy?" I would say that it's the new experience of waking up, walking around, and dealing with life with self-confidence and a *sense of calm*. You may find this hard to believe, but it's a state of mind that I'd never experienced before. Never. Even during the COVID-19 pandemic when I could have been in a constant panic about what was going on and fearing for everyone's health and safety and well-being, I wasn't. I felt an appropriate level of concern—for myself and for others. But also trust and optimism. I was able to access a faith that things were going to be okay. That feeling had never been accessible to me before.

EMDR is the therapy that allowed me to uncover—and under-stand—the dynamics of my development. The story I see now is very different from the one my fractured brain was holding at the beginning of treatment. My invisible wounds had kept me from see-ing and thinking clearly, from fully feeling and knowing the truth.

I now recognize that I experienced childhood attachment trauma and "willful neglect" from a narcissistic mother who was incapable of loving her children. I got crumbs in lieu of a loving relationship and lived in fear of being cut off altogether if I didn't perform and adopt her currency of appearances and status—for me, it was attachment at any cost. The same was true for my narcissistic, bullying father, who convinced me that if I defied, challenged, or surpassed him in any way, there would be a penalty: I would be beaten and banished. This set up a self-sabotaging pattern that was activated, again and again, in my professional and personal lives. I rebelled against men who were my superiors at work, squandered large sums of money, and failed to establish financial security.

The bottom line is that with a *child's mind*, I deduced that I was disliked and unloved because I was not *worthy*, and I subsequently developed a survival strategy of grandiosity to fend off a core belief that I was worthless. Luckily for me, I had a few relationships—with my sisters, my grandmothers, and a handful of teachers—that saved me from turning to more extreme behaviors and self-protective maneuvers. I also had the support, later in life, of dedicated, loyal friends who stayed in touch and supported me even when they didn't understand what I was going through.

I understand now that the neglect I endured at the hands of my mother, starting at birth, combined with her lack of boundaries and hyper-sexualized behaviors—along with the rape by my pediatrician—hijacked my normal psychosexual development and damaged my ability to form trusting, intimate, sexual relationships.

There have been other remarkable changes in my life since I finished my work with Dr. Magnavita. My friendships have become much deeper and more intimate. I used to think my relationships with my friends were as fragile as my relationship with my parents and one argument would mean *losing* that friend, so they had a much more superficial quality. I've since discovered that relationships are resilient and that recognizing and addressing conflict is critical for keeping them honest and authentic. I now realize that working through conflicts can actually make them stronger.

And even though my job was my whole life and sole source of self-esteem during my career, I *never* felt confident in my abilities or talents. Today, I'm running my own communications consulting business and I feel confident about the value I provide to my clients and the unique quality of my work.

I am also starting to understand what dating is all about: spending time with women who interest and attract me, but without the anxiety and panic that used to overwhelm me. As naïve as it may sound, I'm now—in my sixties—learning what most people learn in their teens or twenties about how dating works. It's about spending time with many different potential partners, experiencing various activities and situations—and seeing how it all *feels*. I know I've arrived late to the party, but I'm hopeful that it's not over for me—not yet.

Since I finished my work with Dr. Magnavita, I haven't reexperienced either of the two nightmares that plagued me for decades. And now, like for most people, a public restroom is a godsend—not a harbinger of fear and anxiety.

Finally, and most unexpectedly, I have reconnected with my brother in a new and genuine way after a long separation. He told me that he didn't care how long I had been away. He was just filled with "joy and relief" that we might finally have the chance to be brothers. Since then, I have discovered a person entirely unlike the one who kept me in a constant state of fear throughout my childhood. We are getting to know, understand, and appreciate one another, free from the influence of our parents. It turns out that he had been suffering in similar ways and has now started on his own path of discovery and healing with EMDR therapy.

Today, there are no more pictures in my apartment of my family's opulent homes or my photogenic parents. Instead I keep two pictures of myself on my desk: one from when I was about three years old and one from kindergarten. In the three-year-old's face, I see a blank stare—a child who is lost, with dirt on his face and in dirty clothes. There are no signs whatsoever of being loved, cared for, or attached to *anyone*. In the kindergarten picture, I see a boy, trying hard to smile, who feels alone and afraid. I keep these pictures on my desk so that I have a daily opportunity to think about those younger versions of myself, as if they were alive and with me. I reassure them that I am here for them, to protect them and give them the love, attention, and encouragement that they deserved but never received. When I got discouraged during my thirteen-month battle with my health care company about paying for treatment with Dr. Magnavita, I would regularly regroup and push on, knowing I was fighting for those younger parts of myself who at the time couldn't fight for themselves or find the security and nurturance they deserved.

I practice yoga regularly. During the final pose, Shavasana, I think about *all* those younger parts of me. As I lie there, I imagine each one of them cautiously coming out of hiding, one at a time, walking over to me and letting me hold and comfort them. Eventually, we are all together: One is teary; one is doing that short, shallow hiccup-breathing that kids do when they've been scared or upset but are now safe and protected in their parent's arms; and one just smiles and holds my hand.

They are all grateful to be held and loved and to have been rescued from their isolation.

I will always be grateful to Dr. Magnavita for rescuing me from mine.

An important aspect
of recovery is the healing
and reintegration of
our child selves.

Debbie: When I visited Dr. Magnavita to discuss Michael's journey, he had a lot to say about the markers of Michael's transformation:

Dr. Magnavita: When Michael first came into session, he looked disheveled and neglected, like someone who was not taking care of himself, not eating well, not exercising. He was living in a barren apartment with no food in the refrigerator. What happened in the course of his transformation is that he became increasingly able to engage with his life. As he moved away from being in 24/7 survival mode, new possibilities opened up for him. About halfway through the treatment, he came in and said, "I was actually able to go in and go to the bathroom, in a public restroom, for the first time in my life." That was huge for him.

The next transformation was noted when he began coming to sessions excited because he was actually able to listen to music and hear the lyrics and the melody; then, he was able to repeat them. To me, that represented a profound shift in his information processing system. His system was no longer broken, no longer off-line. I said, "I think, Michael, what's happening is that you'd been taking in all the information from the world through a straw, and now, it's opening up to a funnel." Previously, he only had a very narrow bandwidth, and to get that information in, he had to go over and over and over it.

As it turns out, he actually has an almost photographic memory that had never been functional before. With this shift, he started reading books voraciously. He'd come in and say, "I've been in the park reading. I never knew this story!" He was enthralled with this newfound ability to engage with the world in a way that could actually nourish him. Prior to this, he had never felt fed by music or literature. He only felt compelled; it had simply been about punching a ticket for achievement so he could feel important, worth something, and able to get his mother's approval.

Also, over the course of therapy, he furnished his home and started cooking for himself. He'd come in and tell me about a delicious meal he'd prepared for himself, and how satisfying it was to have homemade food in his freezer, made by him and for him. And he'd talk excitedly about his desire to nurture himself and to explore new domains.

It was very joyous. It was almost like Rip Van Winkle being awakened.

Debbie: Our hope is that we have convinced you that you can—absolutely—heal from the effects of trauma. In my practice, over the course of almost thirty years, I have had the privilege of witnessing major transformations where clients shift from feeling defective and broken and unworthy to feeling extremely compassionate toward themselves and proud of who they are. Over the course of treatment, they come to see themselves as survivors who are deserving of love, success, and happiness. They eventually experience themselves as good—deeply good—and able to make a contribution in the world, within their family, workplace, or community. People report that they're able to make their way feeling calmer, more regulated, and safer. They are less phobic and definitely more courageous. My client Chantel went on to complete her graduate training in social work and joined an organization dedicated to fighting systemic racism; she has a special interest in tackling racial disparities within the criminal justice system.

That is just one example of how, with effective treatment, survivors reach a point where they are no longer fearful of getting panicky or having to flee from situations, and they have a sense of

With EMDR processing,
unhealthy defenses
melt away and new,
healthy behaviors emerge.

having more control and choice. Their internal world is no longer small and disjointed. They are no longer afraid of big feelings and are able to access a range of positive and negative emotions without worry. They no longer feel guilty for surviving or failing to save others. And they eventually come to embrace all aspects of themselves and all aspects of their lives.

I see and hear how people are able to be different in relationships after EMDR therapy. "Finally, I'm able to be myself. I'm not pretending anymore. I don't have to be ashamed of who I am." For the first time in their lives, clients are able to express their needs, use their voices, and share with others how they feel and what they know. And intimacy is within reach—sexual and emotional intimacy. As my forty-five-year-old divorced client said as she began dating again for the first time in twenty years, "If you're able to show up as you are, and trust that you're good enough and worthy of love, it's a whole different ball game." Mark—the man who confronted his ex-wife about having an affair during their marriage—also started to date again. As he began a new relationship, he found that he was able to open his heart and share his vulnerabilities in a way that had never been possible before. He also reported that he was able to ask for what he wanted, without apology or fear of abandonment. He commented again and again that he was now seeing the entirety of his life in a whole new light.

This is not uncommon; toward the end of treatment, clients arrive at a place where, for the first time, they are able to put all the pieces together in a way that makes sense. It's like they finally have their very own "site map"—a coherent narrative or sense of continuity across time. They have a sense of where they've been, where and who they are now, and who they want to be in the future.

By the end of treatment, there's a fluidity to the way peo-ple describe their experience. And there's a sense of ownership. It's more than simply being able to put together all the pieces to tell a story. This is particularly true for those who were abused or neglected as children. They often reach a point where they stop referring to that traumatized child and start speaking from a first-person, "I" perspective. They move from "That happened over there" to "This is *my* story. I was abused. I was abandoned. I was neglected. This is what happened in *my* life, and this is how it affected me." Completing treatment leads to a sense of pride about having survived and learned from challenging life experi-ences. There's often a sense of appreciation for one's resilience and wisdom.

Once people get unhooked from old beliefs, feelings, voices, and memories, they are able to initiate new projects with confi-dence and courage. They no longer see themselves as victims—no longer as survivors, even—but as individuals who can thrive and contribute—creative and powerful, and able to be movers and shakers in the world.

AM I FINISHED OR WILL I NEED TO RETURN TO THERAPY?

My clients always ask me whether their trauma symptoms are going to return. Sometimes symptoms do. If they do, though, they are usually not a surprise and rarely come back with the same vehemence or power as before. It may mean that there is an aspect of their history that we failed to address or, perhaps, we need to revisit a piece of work that we did, with a new plan to look at it from another angle. I tell clients that my door is always open. They are welcome to come back for a session or two or three if they hit a

Successful therapy
offers you a "site map"—
a more accurate narrative
of your life.

place in their life where something from the past starts creeping in again or if they simply need some support with a current situation or traumatic experience.

Sometimes people come back after their kids are more independent, when they can actually do the next level of work, or sometimes, after they retire, when they're finally ready to look at things that they hadn't previously been able or ready to address. But rarely, if ever, do people come back into treatment and find themselves back where they started. Instead, they are typically able to reengage with the work, their trauma history, and their own internal experience with greater insight and resilience. They return with new life experiences that offer valuable, new information and perspectives. And finally, clients come back to treatment to share how they've healed, and how good they feel. For me, there is no greater reward.

7

When You're Ready: Resources to Get You Started on Your EMDR Journey

FINDING AN EMDR THERAPIST

So, what's the first step when you are ready to begin EMDR therapy or are at least curious enough to talk with someone about the possibility of starting EMDR therapy? How do you find a qualified EMDR therapist who is a good fit for you? I would recommend beginning with a visit to the EMDR International Association (EMDRIA) website. EMDRIA is the US-based membership organization for EMDR therapists and is dedicated to maintaining the highest standards of excellence and integrity with regard to the practice of EMDR therapy. As an organization, EMDRIA works to establish and uphold standards of practice, training, certification, and research and to provide information, education, and advocacy for its members and the public. On the EMDRIA website, you can watch some introductory videos about EMDR therapy, hear some client and therapist stories and reflections, and read some more about this exciting psychotherapy. Most importantly, you can use the "Find an EMDR Therapist" directory to locate practitioners in your area.

If you'd like to talk with someone who has the highest level of training and experience, that would be an EMDRIA-approved "Consultant." One level down from there in terms of training and experience are "Certified" therapists. Working with someone who is either a Consultant or a Certified therapist offers you some guarantees about their level of training and experience. That said, it's possible that you may not be able to find available Consultants or Certified therapists in your area or ones who are in-network for your insurance provider, as was the case for Michael. Not all EMDRIA members choose to pursue this higher level of credentialing; it's not required, so don't necessarily discount those without it.

If you are not able to find a qualified EMDR therapist in your area, you may need to look beyond EMDRIA, because not all EMDR-trained therapists join this organization. Many states have local EMDR networks with "Find a Therapist" directories. You can easily search online for networks or regional groups in your area. You can also check out various EMDR training organizations or institutes to see if they provide a list of therapists in your area who have completed one of their basic training programs. For example, the EMDR Institute, started by Dr. Francine Shapiro, offers a "Find a Clinician" list of all the therapists trained within their program over the years. Just a reminder, though: Having completed a basic training in EMDR therapy does *not* guarantee that a therapist is experienced, skillful, or right for you. Keep reading, and please consider the list of questions that we offer as you begin the process of searching for an EMDR therapist for yourself.

One final set of resources: Consider contacting referral services like the American Psychological Association Psychologist Locator service or the Psychology Today "Find a Therapist" service. Also, professional organizations specifically focused on trauma education, research, and treatment—the International Society for the Study of Trauma and Dissociation (ISSTD) and the International Society for Traumatic Stress Studies (ISTSS)—offer "Find a Therapist/Clinician" directories. Links for these and other referral services can be found under Debbie's Recommended Resources in the Websites section on page 274.

If you are reading this book from outside the United States, it is important for you to know that countries or regions around the world often have their own EMDR therapy membership organizations. Each of these organizations has their own referral directory or service. For example, you can contact EMDR Europe, EMDR Canada, EMDR Ibero America, EMDR UK and Ireland, or EMDR Japan, just to name a few. A full listing of EMDR associations around the world can be found on the EMDR Institute website (under "EMDR Organizations").

Finding the right therapist for *you* is critical. Research has indicated that one of the most important factors related to therapy success is the quality of the relationship between the therapist and the client. To start with, you want to look for a therapist who readily responds to your outreach, whether you make contact online or by phone. When you make contact, does the therapist get back to you in a timely manner? Does he show interest in learning about you and the problems for which you are seeking help? Does she take some time with you to help you understand how she works, or what to expect from therapy? It's important to ask about a therapist's training, years of experience, how long she's been doing trauma-informed therapy and more specifically, EMDR therapy, and whether she's worked with other clients with problems similar to yours.

Finding the right therapist

is a process.

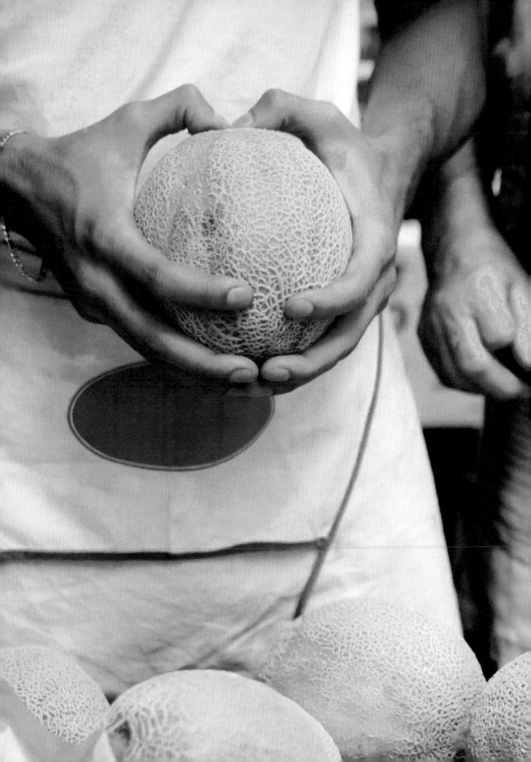

Also, if you have any specific needs or requests, share them with your potential therapist on the phone or in your first session. For example, if you are struggling with sexual or gender identity, you may want to specifically look for an EMDR therapist familiar with LGBTQ issues. If your religion is very important to you or you have a specific spiritual orientation, you may want to see someone who shares that interest or affiliation. I had someone call and say she was looking for a therapist who combines Buddhist meditation, yoga, art therapy, *and* EMDR. Believe it or not, I was able to find the perfect match for her!

Or you may need an EMDR therapist with a particular area of expertise. All EMDR therapists are exposed to a basic training curriculum, but then it's up to the individual therapist to get specialized training above and beyond that initial education. You may be looking for a therapist who has expertise with EMDR and medical illness, phobias, addictions, obsessive compulsive disorder, domestic violence, or issues related to being adopted. As I mentioned in chapter 2, if you are dealing with a severe, complex trauma history and experiencing significant dissociative symptoms (such as blank spells, hearing voices inside your head, depersonalization), it is critical that you see an EMDR therapist with a specialization in evaluating and treating dissociative disorders.

KEY QUESTIONS TO ASK POTENTIAL THERAPISTS

In looking at a therapist's website or talking with him on the phone, trust your gut. Does this person seem kind, attuned, knowledgeable, and professional? On the opposite page are some essential questions to help you discern whether a given therapist is right for you.

- What is your general educational background and training? Are you licensed? Do you have training in trauma-informed therapy beyond your EMDR basic training?

- What is your level of training as an EMDR therapist? Did you complete an EMDRIA-approved training program (or a training program approved by a comparable organization, if outside the US)? How many years have you been practicing EMDR therapy since you completed your basic training? Do you use EMDR therapy on a regular basis in your practice? In a given week, how often do you use EMDR therapy with your clients?

- Are you a member of EMDRIA or another EMDR membership organization? Are you a Certified EMDR therapist or a Consultant? Do you attend the annual EMDRIA conference (or a similar annual conference in your country)? Do you attend advanced trainings in applying EMDR with different problems or populations?

- Have you treated other people like me or with my kinds of problems (for example, domestic violence, racial discrimination, medical trauma, social anxiety, perfectionism, divorce) using EMDR therapy? Have you had advanced training in treating, for example, complex PTSD, eating disorders, dissociative disorders, or addictions?

- Are you trained in other modalities or approaches in addition to EMDR therapy? Can you tell me about how you integrate these approaches in your work with clients?

EMDR therapy is my primary approach to helping my clients, but I integrate many concepts and strategies from other models—internal family systems, sensorimotor psychotherapy, accelerated experiential dynamic psychotherapy, hypnosis, cognitive-behavioral therapy, and dialectical behavior therapy— to facilitate change and healing. And I consistently look through the conceptual lenses of attachment theory, polyvagal theory, affect theory, structural dissociation theory, and interpersonal neurobiology. Some of my colleagues have playfully suggested that I could be diagnosed with MMD—multiple model disorder! Michael's therapist, Dr. Jeffrey Magnavita, is similarly an integrationist, skillfully combining many other modalities with EMDR therapy in his approach. Michael undoubtedly benefited from his broad repertoire of skills and synthesis of models. If you're curious, I'd encourage you to talk with your therapist about the models, theories, and maybe even the research findings that have influenced their work.

In the course of your first session with a potential new therapist, notice how you feel in this person's presence. How is your body and nervous system responding to sitting with this individual? Do you feel safe, at ease, emotionally held? Do you feel seen and heard, understood, and validated? Can you imagine sharing the intimate details of your life with this person? Do you feel comfortable in this therapist's office? If you are working virtually with someone, all of these basic questions and guidelines still apply. Ultimately, do you feel comfortable and pleased with the experience of connecting with this person online?

Even if you feel nervous, shy, or unsure, speak honestly about your struggles and ask questions. Finally, if you are not sure this is the right person for you, *don't hesitate* to talk with or meet with a few more therapists. It is critically important that you take the time up front to find the therapist who is, indeed, the best fit for you.

PRACTICAL QUESTIONS TO ASK YOURSELF AND
YOUR NEW THERAPIST

- How often do you meet with people? How long are your sessions, and what is your fee for a session? Is it possible to do extended sessions? (Talk therapists of various stripes typically do 45- to 60-minute sessions. Though not always necessary, the ideal for EMDR therapy sessions is 60–90 minutes.)

- Do you offer intensive or consecutive-day EMDR treatment?

- Do you offer adjunctive EMDR treatment? In other words, are you willing to see me for EMDR therapy if I still want to continue working with my current therapist?

- Do you offer remote or virtual EMDR sessions?

- Do you accept insurance? If so, which plans do you accept? Can you bill my insurance company directly? If you don't accept my insurance, can you still send claims directly to my health insurance company or provide me with receipts that I can submit so I can use my out-of-network benefits?

- Do you have a sliding fee for people paying out-of-pocket and experiencing financial hardship?

- Ask yourself: Is the location of this therapist's office within reach for me? Can I realistically make it to sessions on a regular basis, or are the challenges (distance, rush-hour traffic, poor public transportation options) too stressful or great?

If you feel like it's going to be hard to get to a particular therapist because their office is far away or too difficult to reach without a car, take that into consideration. You want to set yourself up for success and certainly don't want to be arriving to sessions late, stressed, or exhausted. Michael traveled many, many miles to see Dr. Magnavita, but he was committed to that plan, was self-employed, and had considerable flexibility in his life at the time. Obviously, that's not going to be possible for everyone or even for most people.

ADJUNCTIVE EMDR THERAPY

If the notion of EMDR therapy intrigues you and you're already seeing a therapist, you'll need to decide if you would actually like to try something different. Have you gone as far as you think you can go with your current therapist? Is it time to terminate and make a move? Or do you want to continue to work with your primary therapist and simultaneously do some adjunctive work with an EMDR therapy specialist? If you are not interested in leaving your current therapist, you can likely find an EMDR therapist who will see you while you continue your work with your primary therapist. Typically, adjunctive EMDR therapy is short-term and very goal focused. For those who are struggling with more extreme dysregulated behaviors such as addictions, suicidality, or self-injury; those who are experiencing significant dissociative symptoms; or those who remain quite fearful of emotion, adjunctive therapy may not be an appropriate option, because it generally moves the client into processing traumatic material rather quickly. Most therapists who agree to provide adjunctive EMDR therapy will assume that relevant stabilization work has already taken place in the client's primary therapy.

INTENSIVE EMDR THERAPY

In recent years, more and more EMDR therapists and programs are offering intensive or consecutive-day EMDR therapy. As an alternative to once-a-week therapy, intensive EMDR treatment typically involves meeting with a therapist several hours a day—often in the morning and then again in the afternoon—and sometimes, over the course of consecutive days. In some programs or retreats, EMDR therapy is integrated with other activities such as physical exercise, yoga, or educational classes. There are many advantages to intensive EMDR therapy, including treatment efficiency, reduced risk of treatment being interrupted by life crises, and more rapid relief from symptoms. Research suggests that intensive treatment is safe and effective and can significantly reduce your overall treatment time. It is particularly worth considering if (1) you are looking for more intensive treatment or a higher level of care but don't want to consider hospitalization or a residential treatment program; (2) mental health problems are putting you at risk of losing your job; (3) your life circumstances make it difficult to make it to therapy on a weekly basis; (4) you have an upcoming challenge that you need to be ready for (such as a court date, confrontation with an abuser, performance, or starting college or a new job); or (5) you live far away from your therapist and want to make the most of each visit to reduce the overall length of treatment. Because of the distance (more than two hours from New York City to Glastonbury, Connecticut), Michael typically did two ninety-minute psychotherapy sessions with Dr. Magnavita each time he traveled to see him. Intensive treatment is not going to be possible, appropriate, or affordable for everyone, but you can explore all relevant concerns with any potential EMDR therapist or program intake coordinator.

Yoga, meditation, art,
bodywork, and exercise
can help get your emotional
and thinking brains
back in balance.

INSURANCE

You can contact your insurance company and ask whether they have providers who specialize in trauma-informed treatment or in treating PTSD. If you're lucky, some insurance providers will even be able to tell you if a clinician has more specific trauma treatment expertise working with, for example, veterans, victims of domestic violence, child abuse survivors, or refugees. Clients can ask specifically if there are any EMDR practitioners on their insurance panel. If the insurance company cannot identify any EMDR practitioners, then you can make a case, like Michael did, to have your insurance company cover the cost of treatment with an out-of-network EMDR practitioner. This is often called a "single provider exception" or "single case agreement."

As with any insurance request, it may require perseverance. It took Michael more than a year, with several escalations ("Can I speak to your supervisor?" "Can I speak to *your* supervisor?") through the hierarchy of his insurance company and finally an external appeal review of his case, to get full reimbursement. EMDR therapy is widely recognized as a research-supported, effective treatment for trauma-related disorders and is recommended worldwide in the practice guidelines of US and other international organizations. That said, not all insurance companies are up to date on research findings or international recommendations, so it's important to be ready with some talking points or references related to EMDR's evidence base in the treatment of PTSD and trauma-related difficulties. As a consumer, you have a right to expect your insurance company to enlist therapists who offer the leading evidence-based treatments, and if they are unable to do that, then it is reasonable to expect them to cover treatment with qualified therapists not on their panel. You are entitled to the best, most appropriate services for yourself. If you have found a therapist with whom you'd like to work, be prepared to make a case for why this therapist is precisely the right professional, with the right skills and expertise, to treat you. You can certainly ask a therapist to help you make a case to your insurance company. Often, advocacy from a therapist can make a significant difference (though it may not be something that every therapist is willing or able to do).

COMPLEMENTARY HEALING MODALITIES

For many people, this is a journey back into their bodies—a homecoming of sorts. Their EMDR therapist is one kind of guide on this journey, but for many, it's also helpful to connect with a body-focused teacher or therapist to help ease the way home. Assistance from a massage therapist, dance teacher, yoga instructor, cranial sacral practitioner, or acupuncturist can be invaluable. If something is not moving in our treatment—if some kind of block is impeding progress at an emotional or body level—I sometimes recommend yoga, mindfulness meditation, various types of bodywork, exercise, or neurofeedback. Sometimes I might even suggest incorporating improvisational theater workshops, drumming, or art therapy. These kinds of activities can be quite helpful in getting your nervous system more regulated and your emotional and thinking brains back to working well together.

To comprehensively heal, clients need to be able to tune in to and listen to their bodies, be comfortable in their own skins, and ultimately embrace and work with the stories that their bodies have been holding over the course of their lifetimes. Sometimes

Once released from old
memories, we are no longer
held captive by our past.

these alternative therapies or experiences can help with the process of transforming shame about one's body and ultimately about oneself. Such adjunctive work can enable clients to move from feeling frozen, small, weak, hardened, or constricted to feeling emancipated—able to move more freely and be more open in the world and able to access their truest selves, in words, actions, and expression. As my petite, five-foot tall, mild-mannered client said toward the end of her therapy, "I no longer feel like a nervous little mouse, trying to stay out of sight and in the shadows. I don't exactly feel like a giant, but I definitely feel bigger, stronger, and better able to hold my own in the world." She credits her work with EMDR and her experiences in an improvisational theater troupe for her transformation.

Epilogue

Somewhere in the middle of writing *Every Memory Deserves Respect* together, I sent Michael an email saying that I didn't like some of the initial images he had selected for the book. And since it was late at night and I was tired, I didn't choose my words carefully.

I received a reply from Michael the next day with the subject line "This must be a trigger." He explained that he had felt unsettled and upset when he read that I was unhappy with his recent choices. He acknowledged that my comment had stirred something "old" related to an interaction with a family member. He shared his feelings and reflections in a way that brought up a groundswell of compassion in me. I wanted to understand more and needed him to know how much I truly valued him as my coauthor and collaborator. When we connected by phone, the words came easily for both of us, and we quickly reached a place of understanding.

Why am I sharing this story with you as we approach the final pages of the book? Because I remember being profoundly moved by my interaction with Michael that day as I realized that both of us were benefiting from his two years of hard work in EMDR therapy. Michael recognized that he had been triggered—but he didn't get dysregulated in any big way; he didn't run away, give me the cold shoulder, withdraw, dissociate, freeze, or shift into some other defensive stance. He reached out to me and talked with me directly, honestly, and with vulnerability, not grandiosity. We both showed up for that conversation and emerged from it feeling

When you recognize that you have choices, you can dare to dream—nothing is impossible or out of reach.

pleased with our relationship and excited about our vibrant and creative collaboration. One little conversation reflected a huge amount of healing and a brand-new approach to living and interpersonal relationships.

Our conversation also reminded me that mental health and freedom from one's traumatic past are not just about eliminating symptoms, and EMDR therapy is not just about desensitizing memories and replacing old voices in your head with new, more positive ones. When you dedicate yourself to healing and bring a willingness to go to the mat to save yourself, everything can change. You no longer need to feel powerless, like a victim, trapped by your circumstances, misunderstood, and bullied by those around you. You are able to set limits, use your voice, and advocate for your own happiness and satisfaction. You are no longer at the mercy of your own reactions; instead, you're able to view your emotions as an important source of information and a sign that you are alive and simply responding to the world around you. You begin to see and feel your potential, and, as you resolve your relationships with the people and experiences of your past, you are better able to enjoy your relationships and adventures in the present. You need not worry that you will be thrown off-kilter by any unexpected or unwanted bump in the road. You're able to surrender your outdated defenses and are free to open your heart—to joy, excitement, and love—without debilitating fear.

Our goal in writing this book was to describe the many forms that trauma takes and the ways in which it affects your mind, body, brain, behavior, and *heart*. In particular, we wanted to help you understand the effect of your trauma history on your adult relationships, and how EMDR, experienced within the context of a secure therapeutic relationship, can make all the difference in how you engage with others—in both your professional *and* personal lives.

We hope that you can use what you have learned here to move forward into a new reality for yourself. We each know how much courage and persistence it takes to initiate and stay the course. We both know that you must be lovingly relentless and relentlessly loving with yourself in the process. And, of course, we both know how profound the rewards can be.

We will both be rooting for you.

EMDR is not just about letting go of past burdens, but also about coping better in the present and setting goals for the future.

Debbie's Recommended Resources

Out of all the books and websites available, these are the ones I most regularly loan to my clients or recommend.

EMDR-SPECIFIC BOOKS

Getting Past Your Past
Francine Shapiro; Rodale, 2012

EMDR: The Breakthrough Therapy for Overcoming Anxiety, Stress, and Trauma
Francine Shapiro and Margot Silk Forrest; Basic Books, 2016

Looking Through the Eyes of Trauma and Dissociation: An Illustrated Guide for EMDR Therapists and Clients
Sandra Paulsen; Booksurge, 2009

RECOVERING FROM TRAUMA

The Body Keeps the Score: Brain, Mind, and Body in the Healing of Trauma
Bessel van der Kolk; Penguin, 2014

Trauma and Recovery: The Aftermath of Violence— From Domestic Abuse to Political Terror
Judith L. Herman; Basic Books, 2015

It's Not You, It's What Happened to You: Complex Trauma and Treatment
Christine A. Courtois; Telemachus Press, 2014

*Healing from Trauma: A Survivor's Guide to Understanding
Your Symptoms and Reclaiming Your Life*
Jasmin Lee Cori; Marlowe & Company, 2007

*The Complex PTSD Workbook: A Mind-Body Approach to
Regaining Emotional Control and Becoming Whole*
Arielle Schwartz; Althea, 2016

*A Practical Guide to Complex PTSD: Compassionate Strategies
to Begin Healing from Childhood Trauma*
Arielle Schwartz; Rockridge, 2020

*Journey Through Trauma: A Trail Guide to the 5-Phase Cycle
of Healing Repeated Trauma*
Gretchen L. Schmelzer; Avery, 2018

*Polyvagal Exercises for Safety and Connection:
50 Client-Centered Practices*
Deb Dana; W. W. Norton, 2020

Internal Family Systems Therapy (2nd ed.)
Richard C. Schwartz and Martha Sweezy; Guilford, 2020

*Transforming the Living Legacy of Trauma: A Workbook for
Survivors and Therapists*
Janina Fisher; PESI Publishing & Media, 2021

COPING WITH DISSOCIATION

*Coping with Trauma-Related Dissociation: Skills Training for
Patients and Therapists*
Suzette Boon, Kathy Steele, Onno van der Hart; W. W. Norton, 2011

*Healing the Fragmented Selves of Trauma Survivors:
Overcoming Internal Self-Alienation*
Janina Fisher; Routledge, 2017

LEARNING ABOUT YOUR EMOTIONS AND DEFENSES

It's Not Always Depression: Working the Change Triangle to Listen to the Body, Discover Core Emotions, and Connect to Your Authentic Self
Hilary Jacobs Hendel; Random House, 2018

Living Like You Mean It: Use the Wisdom and Power of Your Emotions to Get the Life You Really Want
Ronald J. Frederick; Jossey-Bass, 2009

ATTACHMENT/ATTACHMENT STYLES

The Power of Attachment: How to Create Deep and Lasting Intimate Relationships
Diane Poole Heller; Sounds True, 2019

Attached: The New Science of Adult Attachment and How It Can Help You Find—and Keep—Love
Amir Levine and Rachel S. F. Heller; TarcherPerigee, 2010

WEBSITES

EMDR International Association
emdria.org

Trauma Recovery/EMDR Humanitarian Assistance Programs
EMDRHAP.org

EMDR Institute
EMDR.com

Francine Shapiro Library
emdria.omeka.net

"How EMDR Works?"
youtube.com/watch?v=hKrfH43srg8

ACEs Connection

acesconnection.com

"Got Your ACE Score?" ACEs Too High

acestoohigh.com/got-your-ace-score

International Society for the Study of Trauma and Dissociation

ISST-D.org

International Society for Traumatic Stress Studies

ISTSS.org

The National Child Traumatic Stress Network

nctsn.org

US Department of Veterans Affairs—National Center for PTSD

ptsd.va.gov

Sidran Institute: Traumatic Stress Education & Advocacy

sidran.org

An Infinite Mind

aninfinitemind.org

MaleSurvivor

malesurvivor.org/for-survivors

CPTSD Foundation

cptsdfoundation.org

Trauma Survivors Network

traumasurvivorsnetwork.org

American Psychological Association—Psychologist Locator

locator.apa.org

Psychology Today—Find a Therapist Service

psychologytoday.com/us/therapists

The Trauma Research Foundation

traumaresearchfoundation.org

Notes

PREFACE

70 percent of adults reported one or more traumas in their lifetime: https://www.cambridge
.org/core/terms. https://doi.org/10.1017/9781107445130.002, p 1.
https://www.cambridge.org/core/terms. https://doi.org/10.1017/9781107445130.010,
p 153.

CHAPTER 1

*EMDR has been intensively studied and proven effective—and efficient—in the treatment
of post-traumatic stress disorder:* ISTSS Guidelines Committee. "Posttraumatic Stress
Disorder Treatment Prevention and Guidelines: Methodology and Recommendations."
(2019). istss.org/getattachment/Treating-Trauma/New-ISTSS-Prevention-and
-Treatment-Guidelines/ISTSS_PreventionTreatmentGuidelines_FNL-March-19-2019
.pdf.aspx.

Khan, A. M. et al. "Cognitive Behavioral Therapy Versus Eye Movement Desensitization
and Reprocessing in Patients with Post-Traumatic Stress Disorder: Systematic Review
and Meta-Analysis of Randomized Clinical Trials." *Cureus 10,* 9 (Sep 4 2018): e3250. doi
.org/10.7759/cureus.3250.

*up to 90 percent of adults who experienced a single traumatic event no longer presenting
with PTSD after only three ninety-minute sessions:* Wilson, S. A. et al. "Fifteen-Month
Follow-Up of Eye Movement Desensitization and Reprocessing (EMDR) Treatment for
Posttraumatic Stress Disorder and Psychological Trauma." *J Consult Clin Psychol 65,* 6
(Dec 1997): 1047–56.

Rothbaum, B. O. "A Controlled Study of Eye Movement Desensitization and Reprocessing
in the Treatment of Posttraumatic Stress Disordered Sexual Assault Victims." *Bull
Menninger Clin 61,* 3 (1997): 317–34.

Shapiro, F. *Eye Movement Desensitization and Reprocessing (EMDR) Therapy: Basic
Principles, Protocols, and Procedures* (3rd ed.). New York: Guilford, 2018.

*Research . . . supports the use of EMDR therapy with people who have experienced . . .
child abuse and neglect:* Chen, R. et al. "The Efficacy of Eye Movement Desensitization
and Reprocessing in Children and Adults Who Have Experienced Complex Childhood
Trauma: A Systematic Review of Randomized Controlled Trials." *Front Psychol 9* (2018):
534.

de Jongh, A. et al. "The Current Status of EMDR Therapy Involving the Treatment of Complex Posttraumatic Stress Disorder." *Journal of EMDR Practice and Research 13*, 4 (2019): 284–90.

Korn, D. L. "EMDR and the Treatment of Complex PTSD: A Review." *Journal of EMDR Practice and Research 3*, 4 (2009): 264–78.

77 percent of traumatized combat veterans were free of PTSD in just twelve sessions: Carlson, J. G. et al. "Eye Movement Desensitization and Reprocessing (EMDR) Treatment for Combat-Related Posttraumatic Stress Disorder." *J Trauma Stress 11*, 1 (1998): 3–24.

EMDR was, without question, more effective than the center's "standard care" in reducing the symptoms of PTSD, coexisting depression, and anxiety: Marcus, S. et al. "Three- and 6-Month Follow-up of EMDR Treatment of PTSD in an HMO Setting." *International Journal of Stress Management 11* (2004): 195–208.

EMDR was not only clinically effective but also the most cost-effective of the eleven trauma therapies evaluated in the treatment of adults with PTSD: Mavranezouli, I. et al. "Cost-Effectiveness of Psychological Treatments for Post-Traumatic Stress Disorder in Adults." *PLoS One 15*, 4 (2020): e0232245.doi.org/10.1371/journal.pone.0232245.

the effects of eight sessions of EMDR therapy compared with eight weeks of taking Prozac for the treatment of PTSD: van der Kolk, B. A. et al. "A Randomized Clinical Trial of Eye Movement Desensitization and Reprocessing (EMDR), Fluoxetine, and Pill Placebo in the Treatment of Posttraumatic Stress Disorder: Treatment Effects and Long-Term Maintenance." *Journal of Clinical Psychiatry 68*, 1 (2007): 37–46.

a reduction or even a complete remission in a wide range of problems and symptoms: Shapiro, F. *Eye Movement Desensitization and Reprocessing (EMDR) Therapy: Basic Principles, Protocols, and Procedures* (3rd ed.). New York: Guilford, 2018.

EMDR therapy is based on the idea that psychological difficulties are related to the brain's failure to adequately process traumatic memories: Shapiro, F. and D. L. Korn. "Eye Movement Desensitization and Reprocessing Therapy." In *Treating Complex Traumatic Stress Disorders in Adults: Scientific Foundations and Therapeutic Models*, edited by Julian D. Ford and Christine A. Courtois, pp. 286–308. New York: Guilford, 2020.

Therapists often refer to these kinds of experiences as "little-t" traumas: Mol, S. S. et al. "Symptoms of Post-Traumatic Stress Disorder After Non-Traumatic Events: Evidence from an Open Population Study." *Br J Psychiatry 186* (2005): 494–9.

only about 20 percent of adult trauma survivors [develop PTSD]: Sidran Institute. "Traumatic Stress Disorder Fact Sheet." sidran.org/wp-content/uploads/2018/11/Post-Traumatic-Stress-Disorder-Fact-Sheet-.pdf.

Many different factors influence one's response to trauma and the likelihood of developing a psychiatric disorder: Courtois, C. A. *It's Not You, It's What Happened to You: Complex Trauma and Treatment.* Dublin, OH: Telemachus Press, 2014.

Almost half of [childhood sexual abuse] survivors are sexually victimized again in the future: Walker, H. E. et al. "The Prevalence of Sexual Revictimization: A Meta-Analytic Review." *Trauma Violence Abuse 20,* 1 (2019): 67–80.

a special report recognizing psychological maltreatment as the most challenging and prevalent form of child abuse and neglect: Hibbard, R. "Psychological Maltreatment." June 29, 2020. pediatrics.org/cgi/doi/10.1542/peds.2012-1552.

Children and adolescents with psychological maltreatment in their backgrounds . . . consistently show equal or worse clinical outcome profiles than kids with exposure to both physical and sexual abuse: Hopper, E. et al. *Treating Adult Survivors of Childhood Emotional Abuse and Neglect.* New York: Guilford, 2019.

"The attachment system can be thought of as the psychological version of the immune system": Lyons-Ruth, K. "The Two-Person Construction of Defenses: Disorganized Attachment Strategies, Unintegrated Mental States, and Hostile/Helpless Relational Processes." *J Infant Child Adolesc Psychother 2* (2003): 105–14.

Systemic or institutional racism is . . . defined as "the systemic distribution of resources, power, and opportunity in our society to the benefit of people who are white and the exclusion of people of color": Solid Ground. "Definition & Analysis of Institutional Racism." Accessed July 4, 2020. solid-ground.org/wp-content/uploads/2015/12/ARI_Definitions -Accountability_Standards.pdf.

Roberts, S. O., and M. T. Rizzo. "The Psychology of American Racism." *American Psychologist* (2020, June 25). Advance online publication. http://dx.doi.org/10.1037 /amp0000642.

RaceForward.org. "What Is Systemic Racism?" raceforward.org/videos/systemic-racism.

Racial trauma, in the form of both macroaggressions . . . and microaggressions: Williams, M. T. et al. "Assessing Racial Trauma within a DSM-5 Framework: The UConn Racial /Ethnic Stress & Trauma Survey." *Practice Innovations 3,* 4 (2018): 242–60.

Williams, M. T. et al. "Assessing PTSD in Ethnic and Racial Minorities: Trauma and Racial Trauma." *Directions in Psychiatry 38,* 3 (2018): 179–96.

The EMDR professional community is strongly committed to dismantling racism: Nickerson, M. I. *Cultural Competence and Healing Culturally Based Trauma with EMDR Therapy: Innovative Strategies and Protocols.* New York: Springer, 2017.

CHAPTER 2

data collected during the early months of the pandemic indicated that more than a third of all Americans were showing signs of clinical depression or anxiety or both: Centers for Disease Control and Prevention. "Early Release of Selected Mental Health Estimates Based on Data from the January–June 2019 National Health Interview Survey." (2019). cdc.gov/nchs/data/nhis/earlyrelease/ERmentalhealth-508.pdf.

The Window of Tolerance: Siegel, D. J. *The Developing Mind: Toward a Neurobiology of Interpersonal Experience.* New York: Guilford, 1999.

Ogden, P. et al. *Trauma and the Body: A Sensorimotor Approach to Psychotherapy.* New York: W. W. Norton, 2006.

Ogden, P., and K. Minton. "Sensorimotor Psychotherapy: One Method for Processing Traumatic Memory." *Traumatology, 6,* 3 (2000): 1-20.

The Change Triangle: Hendel, H. J. *It's Not Always Depression: Working the Change Triangle to Listen to the Body, Discover Core Emotions, and Connect to Your Authentic Self,* p. 15. New York: Random House, 2018.

Malan, D. *Individual Psychotherapy and the Science of Psychodynamics.* London: Butterworth-Heinemann, 1979.

Fosha, D. *The Transforming Power of Affect.* New York: Basic Books, 2000.

trauma survivors . . . meet the criteria for many *different diagnoses:* American Psychiatric Association. *Diagnostic and Statistical Manual of Mental Disorders* (5th ed.). Arlington, VA: American Psychiatric Association, 2013.

World Health Organization. "International Classification of Diseases for Mortality and Morbidity Statistics, 11th Revision." 2018. icd.who.int/browse11/l-m/en.

intrusive symptoms, avoidant symptoms, and hyper-arousal symptoms . . . [are] most commonly associated with the diagnosis of post-traumatic stress disorder: World Health Organization. "International Classification of Diseases for Mortality and Morbidity Statistics, 11th Revision." 2018. icd.who.int/browse11/l-m/en.

the brain is . . . capable of "holding back" memories it deems too potentially debilitating to remember: Hulbert, J. C., and M. C. Anderson. "What Doesn't Kill You Makes You Stronger: Psychological Trauma and Its Relationship to Enhanced Memory Control." *J Exp Psychol Gen 147,* 12 (Dec 2018): 1931–49.

it is not rare at all *for people who were sexually abused in childhood to go for many years, even decades, without having any recognizable or obvious memories of that abuse:* Brewin, C. R. "Autobiographical Memory for Trauma: Update on Four Controversies." *Memory, 15,* 3 (2007): 227–48.

Hopper, J. "Recovered Memories of Sexual Abuse." July 1, 2020. jimhopper.com/recovered -memories-of-sexual-abuse/.

symptoms associated with a diagnosis of complex post-traumatic stress disorder, or C-PTSD: World Health Organization. "International Classification of Diseases for Mortality and Morbidity Statistics, 11th Revision." 2018. icd.who.int/browse11/l-m/en.

For Michael, it was "attachment at any cost": Lipton, B., and D. Fosha. "Attachment as a Transformative Process in AEDP: Operationalizing the Intersection of Attachment Theory and Affective Neuroscience." *Journal of Psychotherapy Integration 21,* 3 (2011): 253–79.

the Adverse Childhood Experiences Study (ACE Study): Felitti, V. J. et al. "Relationship of Childhood Abuse and Household Dysfunction to Many of the Leading Causes of Death in Adults. The Adverse Childhood Experiences (Ace) Study." *Am J Prev Med 14,* 4 (May 1998): 245–58.

The Body Keeps the Score: van der Kolk, B. A. *The Body Keeps the Score: Brain, Mind, and Body in the Healing of Trauma.* New York: Viking, 2014.

The Dissociative Continuum: Fisher, J. *Psychoeducational . . . Aids for Treating Psychological Trauma.* Cambridge, MA: Kendall, 2012.

It helps to think about personality as a great big house, with screen doors between its different rooms: Paulsen, S. *Looking Through the Eyes of Trauma and Dissociation.* North Charleston, SC: Booksurge, 2009.

He had never felt safe enough . . . to begin the process of reengaging with the "exiled" parts of himself: Schwartz, R. C., and M. Sweezy. *Internal Family Systems Therapy* (2nd ed.). New York: Guilford, 2020.

Anderson, F. G. et al. *Internal Family Systems: Skills Training Manual.* Eau Claire, WI: PESI, 2017.

Michael . . . [began] to emerge from his isolation and self-alienation: Fisher, J. *Healing the Fragmented Selves of Trauma Survivors: Overcoming Internal Self-Alienation.* New York: Routledge/Taylor & Francis, 2017.

CHAPTER 3

What happens next starts with a rapid orienting response: Ford, J. D. "Developmental Neurobiology." In *Treating Complex Traumatic Stress Disorders in Adults: Scientific Foundations and Therapeutic Models,* edited by Julian D. Ford and Christine A. Courtois, pp. 286–308. New York: Guilford, 2020.

Ogden, P., and J. Fisher. *Sensorimotor Psychotherapy: Interventions for Trauma and Attachment.* New York: W. W. Norton, 2015.

The Three-Part Brain: MacLean, P. D. *The Triune Brain in Evolution.* New York: Plenum Press, 1990.

Childhood neglect engenders the same fears, perceptions of danger, and feelings of helplessness and despair: Center on the Developing Child, Harvard University. Accessed July 1, 2020, www.developingchild.harvard.edu.

Hopper, E. et al. *Treating Adult Survivors of Childhood Emotional Abuse and Neglect.* New York: Guilford, 2019.

young children affected by neglect and deprivation suffer more pervasive developmental impairments than those exposed to overt physical abuse: Center on the Developing Child, Harvard University. Accessed July 1, 2020. developingchild.harvard.edu.

an incredible quality called neuroplasticity: Doidge, N. *The Brain That Changes Itself: Stories of Personal Triumph from the Frontiers of Brain Science.* New York: Viking, 2007.

"neurons that fire together wire together": Hebb, D. O. *The Organization of Behavior: A Neuropsychological Theory.* New York: Wiley, 1949.

both "top-down" and "bottom-up" approaches to healing: Ogden, P. et al. *Trauma and the Body: A Sensorimotor Approach to Psychotherapy.* New York: W. W. Norton, 2006.

CHAPTER 4

eye movements are the type of bilateral stimulation . . . most supported by research: Shapiro, F. *Eye Movement Desensitization and Reprocessing (EMDR) Therapy: Basic Principles, Protocols, and Procedures* (3rd ed.). New York: Guilford, 2018.

randomized controlled trials support the positive effects of the eye movement component of EMDR: Shapiro, F. *Eye Movement Desensitization and Reprocessing (EMDR) Therapy: Basic Principles, Protocols, and Procedures* (3rd ed.). New York: Guilford, 2018.

most of the attention of researchers and clinicians has been focused on three of these theories: Landin-Romero, R. et al. "How Does Eye Movement Desensitization and Reprocessing Therapy Work? A Systematic Review on Suggested Mechanisms of Action." *Front Psychol 9* (2018): 1395.

Shapiro, F. *Eye Movement Desensitization and Reprocessing (EMDR) Therapy: Basic Principles, Protocols, and Procedures* (3rd ed.). New York: Guilford, 2018.

eye movements are more effective than tones: van den Hout, M. A. et al. "Tones Inferior to Eye Movements in the EMDR Treatment of PTSD." *Behav Res Ther 50,* 5 (2012): 275–9.

the importance of "sequencing" clients' treatment: Herman, J. L. *Trauma and Recovery.* New York: Basic Books, 2015.

Resource development and installation: Korn, D. L., and A. M. Leeds. "Preliminary Evidence of Efficacy for EMDR Resource Development and Installation in the Stabilization Phase of Treatment of Complex Posttraumatic Stress Disorder." *J Clin Psychol 58,* 12 (Dec 2002): 1465–87.

"What was it like for you to experience this? What was it like to do this work with me?": Fosha, D. *The Transforming Power of Affect.* New York: Basic Books, 2000.

the eight-session study of EMDR versus Prozac in the treatment of PTSD: van der Kolk, B. A. et al. "A Randomized Clinical Trial of Eye Movement Desensitization and Reprocessing (EMDR), Fluoxetine, and Pill Placebo in the Treatment of Posttraumatic Stress Disorder: Treatment Effects and Long-Term Maintenance." *Journal of Clinical Psychiatry 68,* 1 (2007): 37–46.

I might even encourage [a client] to stand up and toss a ball with me or push with their hands: Ogden, P., and J. Fisher. *Sensorimotor Psychotherapy: Interventions for Trauma and Attachment.* New York: W. W. Norton, 2015.

getting too "blended" with a younger, traumatized part of themselves: Schwartz, R. C., and M. Sweezy. *Internal Family Systems Therapy* (2nd ed.). New York: Guilford, 2020.

CHAPTER 5

he referred to one's "felt sense.": Gendlin, E. T. *Focusing-Oriented Psychotherapy: A Manual of the Experiential Method. The Practicing Professional.* New York: Guilford, 1996.

People report a range of fears about seeking and starting therapy and then, about actually digging into the process: Steele, K. et al. "Phase-Oriented Treatment of Structural Dissociation in Complex Traumatization: Overcoming Trauma-Related Phobias." *Journal of Trauma and Dissociation 6* (2005): 11–53.

It's . . . not uncommon for there to be significant conflicts between individual parts, each part representing a different survival strategy: Boon, S. et al. *Coping with Trauma-Related Dissociation: Skills Training for Patients and Their Therapists.* New York: W. W. Norton, 2011.

Attachment theory, developed in the 1950s by psychologist John Bowlby: Bowlby, J. *Attachment and Loss.* New York: Basic Books, 1969.

three different insecure attachment styles that remain pretty consistent from childhood into adulthood: Heller, D. P. *The Power of Attachment: How to Create Deep and Lasting Intimate Relationships.* Boulder, CO: Sounds True, 2019.

CHAPTER 7

one of the most important factors related to therapy success is the quality of the relationship between the therapist and the client: Lambert, M. J., and D. E. Barley. "Research Summary on the Therapeutic Relationship and Psychotherapy Outcome." *Psychotherapy: Theory, Research, Practice, Training 38,* 4 (2001): 357–61.

Research suggests that intensive treatment is safe and effective and can significantly reduce your overall treatment time: Bongaerts, H. et al. "Intensive EMDR to Treat PTSD Patients with Severe Comorbidity: A Case Series." *Journal of EMDR Practice and Research 11,* 2 (2017): 84–95.

Greenwald, R. "Get Better Faster! (for Real)," 2013. childtrauma.com/blog/get-better-faster.

Greenwald, R. "The Economic Value of Intensive Trauma Therapy," 2015. childtrauma.com/blog/economic.

I sometimes recommend yoga: Fay, D. *Attachment-Based Yoga & Meditation for Trauma Recovery: Simple, Safe, and Effective Practices for Therapy.* New York: W. W. Norton, 2017.

I sometimes recommend . . . neurofeedback: Fisher, S. F. *Neurofeedback in the Treatment of Developmental Trauma: Calming the Fear-Driven Brain.* New York: W. W. Norton, 2014.

These kinds of activities can be quite helpful in getting your nervous system more regulated: van der Kolk, B. A. *The Body Keeps the Score: Brain, Mind, and Body in the Healing of Trauma.* New York: Viking, 2014.

Acknowledgments

We wish to thank Suzie Bolotin, publisher and editorial director at Workman Publishing, for being so receptive to the idea for this book from the moment Michael first presented it to her, and for actively encouraging him to pursue it in their very first conversation. We are deeply indebted to Mary Ellen O'Neill for being that rare editor who sees and protects the big conceptual picture while also offering painstaking line-by-line editing, all in the service of helping us create a book that moves people and gives them hope. Her generosity, direct yet sensitive feedback, and enthusiasm continually inspired us to strive to make our book better. And we extend our gratitude to everyone at Workman for all they did to create this book and get it into as many hands as possible, especially Kim Daly, Sarah Smith, Barbara Peragine, Rebecca Carlisle, Moira Kerrigan, Ilana Gold, Cindy Lee, and the entire sales team. In addition to our Workman crew, we were fortunate to have Nicola Kraus on our team, guiding us as a veteran writer and helping us with editing and decision-making. Nicola was always there when we needed her, with supportive words, novel solutions to dilemmas, and just the right editorial touch.

Many of the photographs in this book were generously donated by film directors and photographers from Malaysia, Germany, Spain, Denmark, Mexico, and the United States. They donated their photographs because they wanted to be part of this effort to help trauma survivors all over the world. We were touched by their bigheartedness.

Michael: I'd like to thank Debbie for agreeing to join me in this mission. Debbie, your expertise, work ethic, and unflinching attention to detail are world-class . . . but your empathy and humanity are what define you in my mind. I'm grateful to have experienced them both and so honored to have had you as my partner in creating this book.

Thank you to Stever, Elsie, David, and Molly for your enthusiasm for this project from the very beginning. To Tom, Jeff, and Larry for your interest and feedback. To my dearest friend Carol for her love and support right up to her very last day on Earth. And to Reyn for reading every iteration of this manuscript, scrutinizing every photograph and caption, and making some brilliant suggestions which made this book better.

To Dr. Jeffrey Magnavita, thank you for being the champion I never had.

Debbie: I'd like to thank Michael for inviting me to join him on his incredibly important mission. Michael, your mission quickly became my mission. I recall that early in our time together, I taught you the Yiddish word *beshert*. This word literally means "destiny" but is often used when describing something that feels meant to be or inevitable. I shared this word with you in a moment when we were both unexpectedly struck by the good fit and ease of our new partnership. It was a moment of gratitude and delight. I have been moved again and again by your trust in me and by the mutuality of our collaboration. And I have grown to deeply appreciate your courage and creativity, and the passion that you bring to everything you do.

I'd also like to express my appreciation to Jeffrey Magnavita for encouraging Michael to reach out to me as he started to search for a collaborator, and for taking the time to talk with me about his clinical work with Michael, sharing his perspective on his trauma history, struggles, and triumphant healing journey.

I was so touched by everyone who graciously agreed to read early versions of our manuscript and then offered honest, insightful, and incredibly valuable feedback. From my heart to yours, thank you: Marsha, Rae, Jennifer, Lana, Janina, Oliver, Carol, Judy, Nancy, Catherine, Deany, Susan, Charis, Sasha, Louise, and Deb.

On the home front, I am lucky to have a husband who supports all of my initiatives and is always willing to lend a helping hand. As a senior cognitive neuroscientist and sleep researcher, an author and teacher, and a loving partner, Bob offered multiple kinds of help along the way—editing, formatting, and tech and scholarly support as well as much-needed emotional support. He held down the fort at home when I needed time to attend to writing. He helped me recognize that I had something valuable to offer and that I shouldn't hesitate to speak directly from my personal, lived experience as a trauma therapist. Bob, thanks for loving me unconditionally and for always believing in me.

Many people have played a role in my professional development and learning; I have felt their presence at my side throughout the writing of this book. I'd like to thank my EMDR colleagues, particularly those connected with the EMDR Institute, for their friendship and support over the years. I honor them for their professional integrity and determination. Because of their dedication and commitment to healing, with their clients and through their educational and research efforts, EMDR therapy has received the kind of recognition that it deserves as a top-tier trauma treatment. I have also had the good fortune to train with so many incredibly gifted teachers outside the EMDR community—Bessel van der Kolk, Judith Herman, Colin Ross, Diana Fosha, Marsha Linehan, Richard Schwartz, Pat Ogden, and Daniel Brown, just to name a handful who have had a lasting effect on the quality of my work as a trauma therapist. Without a doubt, though, my greatest teachers have been my clients. Because of their willingness to invite me into their lives and their courage in sharing their struggles with me, I have matured as a clinician and grown as a human being. They have inspired me to keep learning, keep healing parts of myself, and keep exploring effective applications for EMDR therapy. My clients are represented here within this book as I have included many of their stories and actual quotes from our sessions.

Last but certainly not least, there is Dr. Francine Shapiro. In June 2019, we lost an academic genius, an out-of-the box thinker, and a warrior in the fight to end suffering in this world. I lost my close friend and mentor. Francine always believed in me, as a therapist and as a teacher, and always showed me the utmost respect. She regularly said that she wanted to learn from me; of course, this baffled me, since, in my mind, I was just a kid and she was a great big famous grown-up. Francine and I were writing a chapter together for a professional book on treating complex traumatic stress disorders when she died. I had just talked with her about the proposal for this book two weeks earlier. She was quite excited about it, to say the least. Meeting Francine changed my life, and learning EMDR has allowed me to help many others change theirs. There are simply no words to capture the depth of my gratitude to her.

Appendix

WHAT IS YOUR ACE SCORE?

Initially developed at Kaiser Permanente, this ten-question inventory of adverse childhood experiences (ACEs) has become an international guide for therapists, doctors, and clients/patients looking to quickly map a person's trauma history.

The inventory focuses on three types of ACEs—abuse, neglect, and household dysfunction—and each affirmative answer counts as one point. That means that a person who was physically abused, with one alcoholic parent and another in the penal system, would have an ACE score of three.

Of course, as we have explored in this book, there are many types of trauma. This inventory includes only these ten because they were mentioned most often by the initial research participants.

The most important thing to remember as you answer these questions is that the ACE score is meant only as a guideline to aid you and your therapist in your healing journey. If you have been exposed to other kinds of adverse experiences over the years, then your risk of health consequences may actually be higher than your ACE score suggests.

Before your eighteenth birthday:

1. Did a parent or other adult in the household often or very often . . . swear at you, insult you, put you down, or humiliate you? Or act in a way that made you afraid that you might be physically hurt?

No ___ **Yes** ___

2. Did a parent or other adult in the household often or very often . . . push, grab, slap, or throw something at you? Or ever hit you so hard that you had marks or were injured?

No ___ **Yes** ___

3. Did an adult or person at least five years older than you ever . . . touch or fondle you or have you touch their body in a sexual way? Or attempt or actually have oral, anal, or vaginal intercourse with you?

No ___ **Yes** ___

4. Did you often or very often feel that . . . no one in your family loved you or thought you were important or special? Or that your family didn't look out for each other, feel close to each other, or support each other?

No ___ **Yes** ___

5. Did you often or very often feel that . . . you didn't have enough to eat, had to wear dirty clothes, and had no one to protect you? Or your parents were too drunk or high to take care of you or take you to the doctor if you needed it?

No ___ **Yes** ___

6. Were your parents ever separated or divorced?

No ___ **Yes** ___

7. Was your mother or stepmother . . . often or very often pushed, grabbed, or slapped, or did she have something thrown at her? Was she sometimes, often, or very often kicked, bitten, hit with a fist, or hit with something hard? Or ever repeatedly hit over at least a few minutes or threatened with a gun or knife?

No ___ **Yes** ___

8. Did you live with anyone who was a problem drinker or alcoholic, or who used street drugs?

No ___ **Yes** ___

9. Was a household member depressed or mentally ill, or did a household member attempt suicide?

No ___ **Yes** ___

10. Did a household member go to prison?

No ___ **Yes** ___

Give yourself one point for each Yes answer. Now add up the total. This is your ACE score.

To read more about how to understand your ACE score, visit the Aces Too High News website (https://acestoohigh.com/got-your-ace-score) and check out the section entitled, "Now that you've got your ACE score, what does it mean?"

Photo Credits

1.	SHAME	© Rainer 81 / Shutterstock
7.	PARIS	© Sergio Azenha / Alamy Stock Photo
15.	GRAVITY	© Bairon Rivera
19.	PHOBIAS	© catinsyrup / iStock
23.	CLEAR OUT	© Chiyacat / Shutterstock
27.	HEAL	© Prostock-Studio / iStock
35.	FROZEN	© Anders Leth Damgaard
41.	SECURE	© Michael Baldwin
45.	ATTACHMENT	© Lee Hudson / Alamy Stock Photo
49.	GENERATIONS	© PhotoAlto sas / Alamy Stock Photo
53.	WITHDRAW	© Rido / Adobe Stock
57.	ADAPT	© RZ Images / Alamy Stock Photo
67.	THERMOSTAT	© Moja Msanii / Unsplash
77.	TREE	© Laura Lee Cobb / Adobe Stock
81.	WHAC-A-MOLE	© Cindy Rae-Tucker
85.	VISIBLE WOMAN	© Molly Bell
89.	DISSOCIATION	© Pol Úbeda Hervàs
93.	HIDING	© Cavan Images / Adobe Stock
97.	BLAME	© 3D Stock Illustrations / Alamy Stock Photo
103.	REPORT CARD	© Michael Baldwin
107.	RISKY	© Cavan / Alamy Stock Photo
111.	BUOYS	© Alex Blåjan / Unsplash
113.	BRAIN DRAWING	© Merchant Mechanics
115.	BROKEN LEG	© jittawit21 / Shutterstock
119.	BRAIN	© Science Source Images
123.	NEGLECT	© Science History Images / Alamy Stock Photo
127.	OVERLOADED	© Quality Stock / Alamy Stock Photo
133.	MAGNETIC	© Alchemy / Alamy Stock Photo

137.	FREEZE	© WildMedia / Adobe Stock
141.	LIMITED	© TMI / Alamy Stock Photo
147.	EMDR	© Javier Ríos
151.	BLS	© John Simoncelli
157.	MAZE	© Martin Bond / Alamy Stock Photo
161.	DEFUSE	© Darkened Studio / Alamy Stock Photo
167.	UNLOCK	© francescoch / iStock
171.	NEW CIRCUITS	© Shepherd Chabata / Alamy Stock Photo
177.	CONTAINERS	© Viktoriia Dogdu / Shutterstock
181.	TARGET	© Gemma Evans / Unsplash
	FAMILY	© Michael Baldwin
185.	SCENERY	© kuzsvetlaya / Shutterstock
191.	DO-OVER	© Thao Le Hoang / Unsplash
195.	TRANSFORM	© Chris Howes/Wild Places Photography / Alamy Stock Photo
203.	DREAMS	© Ethan Hu / Unsplash
207.	A SMELL	© Himanshu Dewangan / Unsplash
	A VOICE	© Shahin Khalaji / Unsplash
	A COLOR	© Cesar Rincon / Unsplash
211.	INTOLERABLE	© Kamira / Shutterstock
215.	BEGINNERS	© Iiana Mikah / Unsplash
221.	PARABLE	© MeSamong / Shutterstock
229.	TRUST	© Satoshi-K / iStock
233.	STYLES	© Izabelle Acheson / Unsplash
239.	REINTEGRATION	© Hongqi Zhang / Alamy Stock Photo
243.	THAW	© AYImages / iStock
247.	SITE MAP	© Fallon Michael / Unsplash
253.	THERAPIST	© Design Pics Inc / Alamy
261.	YOGA	© Madison Lavern / Unsplash
265.	RELEASED	© Timothy Allen / Getty Images
269.	ABUNDANCE	© Kenny Chai
273.	LETTING GO	© masterzphotofo / Adobe Stock

Index

A

ACE Study ten-question inventory, 289–291
Aces Too High News website, 292
achievement, compulsion toward, 13
addictions/addictive behaviors, 24, 30, 72, 78–79, 80, 83, 121, 158, 172, 258
adjunctive EMDR, 257, 258
adult survivors of trauma, 38–39
Adverse Childhood Experiences Study (ACE Study), 83, 86, 289–291
alterations in attention and consciousness, 90
alienation, sense of, 95, 98
aloneness, profound, 95, 98
American Academy of Pediatrics, 39
American Psychiatric Association, 21
American Psychological Association's Psychologist Locator service, 250
amygdala, 31, 115, 118, 120–121
Angelou, Maya, 105
anxious/preoccupied attachment, 230
assessment phase, 163, 175–182
attachment
    anxious/preoccupied, 230
    at any cost, 82, 235
    author and, 82
    avoidant/dismissive, 230
    disorganized, 230–231
    injuries involving, 39
    insecure, 227, 230–231
    role of early, 39–51
    secure, 42–43, 227
    trauma, 37, 234
attachment styles
    anxious/preoccupied, 230
    avoidant/dismissive, 230
    disorganized, 230
    secure, 227, 231
    understanding, 226–231
attention, dual, 149, 169, 172, 187

attentional dysregulation, 86–94, 135
authentic self, 63*fig*
avoidant symptoms, 68, 70–71, 72–73
avoidant/dismissive attachment, 230

B

Baldwin, Michael, personal story of, 8–11, 12–13, 16–17, 54–55, 111, 114
behavioral dysregulation, 75, 78–79, 135
bilateral stimulation (BLS), 148–149, 153, 154, 182–183
Body Keeps the Score, The (van der Kolk), 83, 86
body scan phase, 163, 196–197
body's reaction to trauma, 83–86
bottom-up approaches, 144–145
boundaries, poor, 100–101, 104
Bowlby, John, 226
brain
    childhood neglect and, 121–125
    early stages of trauma processing in, 120–121
    evolution and, 29
    memory and, 125–135
    three parts of, 114–115, 115*fig*
    during a traumatic event, 114–119
bullying, of author, 9, 12

C

Centers for Disease Control and Prevention, 83
Change Triangle, 60, 63, 63*fig*, 64–65, 74, 75
childhood neglect, brain and, 121–125
children
    experience of trauma and, 4, 21, 24, 36, 38–39, 58, 83, 121, 124–125, 139, 199, 245. *See also* Baldwin, Michael
    health problems and adverse experiences of, 83, 86

chronic states of freeze, fight, flight, and collapse (shutdown or immobilization), 117

closure phase, 163, 197–198

codes of silence, 43, 46

collapse (shutdown or immobilization) state/response, 64, 74, 79, 87, 91, 117, 124, 138

complementary healing modalities, 263, 266

complex interpersonal trauma, 37–39, 71, 74

complex post-traumatic stress disorder (C-PTSD, complex PTSD), 68, 74, 90*fig*, 91, 117, 121, 164, 222

compulsive behaviors, 72, 78, 128

conflict, relationships and, 79, 82, 235–236

consecutive-day EMDR therapy, 259

consultants, 250

coping strategies, 72–73

core emotions, 63*fig*, 64–65

coronavirus pandemic, 58–59, 154

"cover stories," 142

D

death
feigned, 87, 119
of perpetrator, 59

defenses, 63*fig*, 64–65, 75, 138, 242, 270

depersonalization, 91

depression
EMDR effectiveness for, 21, 24
poor self-care and, 99
rates of during pandemic, 59
relational dysregulation and, 79
relief from, 173

derealization, 91

desensitization phase, 163, 182–193

developmental repair, 193

developmental trauma, 37

diagnoses, formal, 65–68

disorganized attachment, 230–231

dissociation, 86–94, 100, 108, 117, 121, 135, 138, 158

Dissociative Continuum, 90–91, 90*fig*, 94

dissociative disorders, 68, 90*fig*, 91, 94, 117, 121, 158, 198, 222, 230, 254, 255

dissociative identity disorder (DID), 90*fig*, 94

"do-overs," 188

dual attention, 149, 169, 172, 187

dysregulation
attentional, 86–94, 135
behavioral, 75, 78–79, 135
eating and, 99–100
emotional, 74–75, 135
relational, 79, 82, 135
sleeping habits and, 99–100
somatic, 83–86, 135

E

early attachment, role of, 39–51

eating, dysregulated, 72, 99–100

EMDR International Association (EMDRIA), 249–250

EMDRIA-approved consultants, 250

emotional abuse and neglect, 30, 32, 39. *See also* children: experience of trauma and; neglect

emotional brain, 114–115, 115*fig*, 119, 138–139, 152

emotional dysregulation, 74–75, 135

emotions
ability to access, 244, 270
attachment and, 39, 230
core, 42, 63*fig*, 64–65
EMDR approach and, 43, 145, 149, 152, 154–155, 179, 183, 187–188, 218
inability to access, 55 58
inhibitory, 63*fig*, 64–65
overwhelming/intolerable, 25, 32, 75, 139
regulating, 43
TICES framework and, 175

explicit memory system, 125–129

Eye Movement Desensitization and Reprocessing (EMDR) therapy
adjunctive, 258
basis for, 24–25
brief description of, 145
consecutive-day, 259
description of, 148–152
development of, 20
different therapies and, 219–223
fears regarding, 223–226
finding therapist for, 249–254
intensive, 259
overview of, 155–162

phases of, 162–198
practical questions for yourself and
    therapist, 257–258
processing and, 154–155
PTSD and, 21, 24
questions before pursuing,
    212–219
questions for potential therapists,
    254–256
research on efficacy of, 20–21, 24
eye movements
    compared to tones, 154
    models/theories explaining role of,
        152–153
    research on effects of, 149, 152

F

failure to initiate, 98–99
fear
    of heights, 16
    of intimacy, 13, 16
    of public restrooms, 16
fears regarding therapy, 223–226
feeder memories, 186
"feigned death" reaction, 87, 119
"felt sense," 216–217
fight-or-flight response, 31
flight state/response, 117, 120, 224
floatback technique, 154, 175, 178, 200
freeze state/response, 87, 116, 117, 120,
    136–137, 138, 165, 224
future template, 199

G

Gendlin, Eugene, 216

H

healing, 25, 28
health problems, adverse childhood
    experiences and, 83, 86
Hebb, Donald, 131
heights, fear of, 16
Hendel, Hilary Jacobs, 63
history taking and treatment planning phase,
    162, 163–165
hope, loss of, 98–99
hyper-arousal, 61, 61fig, 62, 68, 71, 138

hypo-arousal, 61, 61fig, 62, 138
hypothalamus, 115, 118, 120–121

I

implicit memory system, 125–129
inhibitory emotions, 63fig, 64–65
insecure attachment, 227, 230–231
installation phase, 163, 193–196
instinctual brain, 114–115, 115fig, 118, 119
institutional racism, 46–47
institutional trauma, 43, 46
insurance, 262–263
integrationists, 256
intensive EMDR, 259
International Society for Traumatic Stress
    Studies (ISTSS), 21, 251
International Society for Treatment of
    Trauma and Dissociation (ISSTD), 251
intimacy, fear of, 13, 16
intrusive symptoms, 68–70
isolation, 95, 98
It's Not Always Depression (Jacobs Hendel), 63

K

Kaiser Permanente, 83, 290
Korn, Deborah, background of, 17, 20, 24, 28

L

language, difficulties with, 54–55
Leeds, Andrew, 168
limit setting, 100–101, 104
little-t traumas, 33
Lyons-Ruth, Karlen, 42–43

M

macroaggressions, 46–47
Magnavita, Jeffrey, 8, 50, 98, 148, 153, 159,
    240–241, 256
medication, 173–174
memories, holding back of, 70
memory
    activating, 175–182
    components of, 31, 31fig, 176–177, 178
    EMDR therapy and, 134–135, 139
    feeder, 186
    "felt sense" and, 216–217
    frozen, 130–131

nature of, 125–129
normal processing of, 129–130
placing in context, 217–218
processing during therapy, 182–193
mental escape routes, 86–94
#MeToo movement, 82
microaggressions, 46–47
multiple personality disorder. *See*
dissociative identity disorder (DID)

N

National Institute of Mental Health, 24
negative self-concept, 95
neglect, 21, 30, 32, 37, 38, 39, 82, 83, 117,
121–125
neurobiology of recovery, 135–139
neuroplasticity, 131–135
9/11, 58

O

omission, acts of, 38
open-hearted state, 63*fig*
optimal arousal state, 138
optimal arousal zone, 61*fig*, 62, 213
Orienting Response model, 152
orienting response, rapid, 116

P

pandemic, 58–59, 154
parasympathetic nervous system, 120, 138,
152
perpetrator, death of, 59
persona, construction of, 11
Phases of EMDR therapy
assessment phase, 163, 175–182
body scan phase, 163, 196–197
closure phase, 163, 197–198
desensitization phase, 163, 182–193
history taking and treatment planning
phase, 162, 163–165
installation phase, 163, 193–196
preparation phase, 162, 165–174
reevaluation phase, 163, 198
"playing possum" reaction, 87, 119
post-traumatic stress disorder/symptoms
(PTSD), 21, 24, 36, 68, 90*fig*, 91, 99, 112,
117, 118–119, 121, 125, 173, 174, 189

power and control, 186–187
preparation phase, 162, 165–174
privilege, 50
processing in EMDR therapy session,
154–155, 182–197
professional organizations, 250–251
promiscuity, 104–105
psychological maltreatment, 39, 42
Psychology Today "Find a Therapist" service,
250
public restrooms, fear of, 16
purpose, loss of, 98–99

R

racism/racial trauma, 46–47
recovery, neurobiology of, 135–139
reevaluation phase, 163, 198
referral services, 250–251
relational dysregulation, 79, 82, 135
relationships, resilience of, 235–236
REM Sleep model, 152
resilience, 105, 110
resource development and installation (RDI),
168–169
resources, 274–277
responsibility and defectiveness, 186–187
risk taking, excessive, 104–105

S

safe place imagery, 168–169
safety and vulnerability, 186–187
secure attachment, 42–43, 227
self-care, poor, 99–100
self-concept, negative, 95
self-injury, 78
self-regulation, 42–43, 139, 172–173, 227
sequencing treatment, 155–162
shame, 78
Shapiro, Francine, 20, 149, 152, 250
shutdown, state of. *See* collapse or shutdown
(shutdown or immobilization) state/
response, shutdown state/response
Siegel, Daniel, 60
silence, codes of, 43, 46
sleeping habits, dysregulated, 99–100
somatic dysregulation, 83–86, 135
stabilization strategies, 168–173

stress hormone levels, 83, 118
sympathetic nervous system, 118, 120, 138, 152
symptoms
    avoidant, 68, 70–71
    hyper-arousal, 61, 62, 68, 71, 74
    hypo-arousal, 61, 62
    intrusive, 68–70
    trauma-based, 68–90
systemic racism, 46–47
systemic trauma, 43, 46

T

talk therapy, limitations of, 142–145
thinking brain, 114–115, 115*fig*, 118, 119, 139
three-part brain, 115*fig*
TICES framework, 175
top-down approaches, 143–144
transformation, promise of, 234–248
trauma
    adult survivors of, 38–39
    attachment, 37, 234
    big-*T*, 32, 58–59, 68, 178
    body's reaction to, 83–86
    brain and, 114–119, 120–121
    catching up with us, 55, 58–60
    children and experience of, 4, 21, 24, 36,
        38–39, 58, 83, 121, 124–125, 139, 199,
        245. *See also* Baldwin, Michael
    complex interpersonal, 37–39, 71, 74
    description of, 28–32
    developmental, 37

    elements of, 32–37
    examples of experiences of, 30
    institutional, 43, 46
    little-*t*, 33
    racism/racial, 46–47
    relational, 37
    responses to, 36–37
    symptoms based on, 68–90
    systemic, 43, 46
treatment planning. *See* history taking and
    treatment planning phase
trigger warnings, 5
triggers
    current, 182–193
    description of, 31–32
    impact of, 58–60
    neuroplasticity and, 134

U

US Department of Defense, 21
US Department of Veterans Affairs, 21

V

van der Kolk, Bessel, 83, 86
visual cortex, 118

W

window of tolerance, 60–63, 61*fig*, 65, 74, 139,
    187, 213
Working Memory model, 153
World Health Organization, 23